OUR World
OCEAN WORLD

Tony Rice

HAMLYN

Series Editor: Julia Gorton
Editors: Jodi Block and Anne Civardi
Designers: Mei Lim and Pauline Bayne
Design Assistant: Stephen Fraser
Art Editor: Rowena Alsey
Picture Research: Elizabeth Weiley
Typesetter: Kerri Hinchon
Production: Sarah Schuman

Cover illustration by Andrew Beckett/Garden Studio
Additional illustrations by Dale Edna Evans,
Bernard Thornton Artists (John Francis, Colin Newman, Bob Bampton),
Garden Studio (Andrew Beckett), Martin Knowelden,
Chris Forsey, Tony Roberts, Peter Sarson, Mike Saunders,
Mick Gillah, Colin Rose, David Ashby, Shirley Mallinson

Published in 1991 by
Hamlyn Children's Books,
part of Reed International Books Ltd.,
Michelin House, 81 Fulham Road,
London SW3 6RB

© Reed International Books Limited 1991

British Library Cataloguing in Publication Data for this book is
available from the British Library.

Although all reasonable care has been taken in the preparation
of this book, neither the Publishers, contributors or editors can
accept any liability for any consequence arising from the use
thereof or from the information contained therein.

ISBN 0 600 57479 2

Typeset in Bembo
Linotronic Output by Tradespools Ltd, Frome, Somerset
Origination by Mandarin Offset, Hong Kong
Produced by Mandarin Offset, Hong Kong

Contents

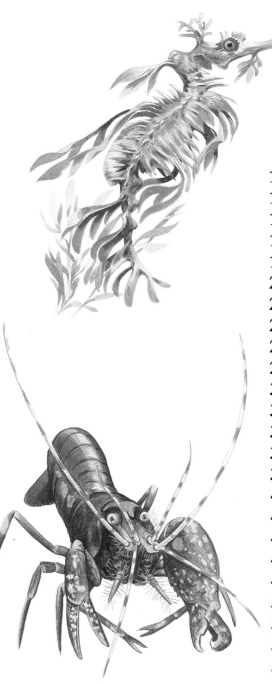

4 The Great Oceans
6 On the Move
8 Rising and Falling
10 Life in the Oceans
12 Plants of the Sea
14 The Floating World
16 Ocean Drifters
18 The World of Fish
20 On the Seabed
22 Life Between the Tides
24 Life in the Shallows
26 The Twilight Zone
28 Down in the Depths
30 Colourful Coral Reefs
32 Under the Ice
34 Hot Water Springs
36 A Way of Life
38 Special Defences
40 Perfect Partners
42 A Sea of Sharks
44 Incredible Journeys
46 A Family of Whales
48 People and the Sea
50 Exploring the Oceans
52 Fishing
54 Farming the Seas
56 Resources of the Sea
58 Polluting the Sea
60 The Future of the Oceans
62 Glossary
63 Index

The Great Oceans

The oceans cover over seven-tenths of the surface of the Earth. They are warmed by the hot tropical Sun and cooled by great sheets of ice at the North and South Poles. They are blown by the wind to form waves and strong currents and pulled by the Moon to produce the tides. They also cover huge underwater mountain ranges, erupting volcanoes, and deep, dark trenches.

Sometimes the oceans can be very destructive, sinking ships and smashing harbour walls, and even buildings built close to the coast. But they also provide people with food and help to control their weather, wherever they live, even if it is far away from the sea.

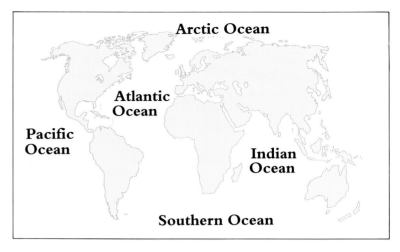

Deep Down
Within a few kilometres of the coast, the oceans are no more than about 200 m (650 ft) deep. Farther away from the land, they become much deeper and the average depth drops to almost 4 km (2.5 miles).

Salty Water
Unlike water in rivers and lakes, seawater contains lots of salt. In most parts of the ocean, each litre (0.22 gallons) of water contains about five heaped teaspoons. Most of it is just like the salt people sprinkle on food.

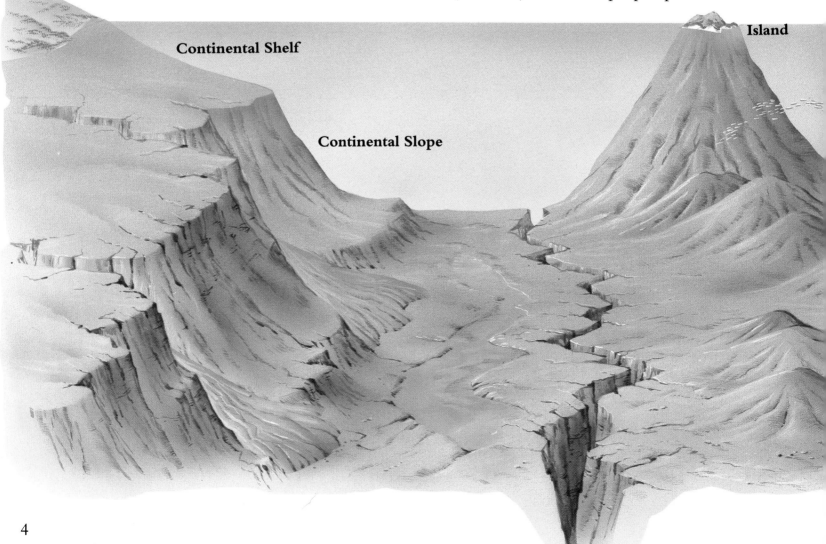

Mainland

Continental Shelf

Continental Slope

Island

Sun's Rays

Sunlit Zone
200 m (650 ft)

Twilight Zone
1,000 m (3,300 ft)

Dark Zone
6,000 m (19,500 ft)

Teeming with Life

Although the oceans are stormy, cold and dark, they are teeming with life, from tiny plants and animals much smaller than a pinhead to the great blue whale.

Volcano

In the Dark

Sunlight cannot pass easily through water. Even in the clearest waters, no sunlight reaches down farther than a few hundred metres. Sea plants, which need sunlight, can only survive near the surface.

Chilly Waters

Under the heat of the tropical Sun, the sea temperature can reach 30°C (86°F) or more. But the Sun warms up only the top layers of water. Even in the hottest parts of the world, water deeper than a few hundred metres is no warmer than 3°C (37°F). Around the Poles, even the surface waters may be as cold as -2°C (29°F).

Ocean Facts

If the oceans were divided equally among all the people on Earth, each person would have about 400 million tonnes of water.

The average temperature of all the seawater in the world is about 5°C (41°F), not much warmer than the inside of a fridge.

The deepest parts of the oceans are in long, narrow trenches. Most of them are in the western parts of the main oceans. The deepest of all is the Marianas Trench in the Pacific, which is over 11,000 m (36,200 ft) deep.

The oceans contain about 9 million tonnes of gold.

Trench

Mountain Range

On the Move

The oceans always seem to be moving except on very calm days. The most easily seen movements are caused by surface waves which can toss about, and sometimes sink, the largest ships. They can also cause terrible damage when they crash on to the shore. Waves are caused by wind blowing across the surface of the sea.

The stronger the wind and the longer it blows in the same direction, the bigger the waves and the faster they travel. Usually the worst storms produce waves no more than 20 m (66 ft) high, but sometimes there are "freak" waves. The biggest wave ever recorded, sighted in the Pacific, measured 34 m (112 ft) high.

Goblin's Kidneys

In the 1500s, sailors realized that their sailing ships were carried along by the ocean currents. When they crossed the North Atlantic, the westward journey was much slower than the return journey if they sailed along the Gulf Stream.

Long before that, large beans called goblin's kidneys (because of their shape) were mysteriously washed up on the shores of western Ireland. The large beans had fallen into the sea from trees on islands in the Caribbean and had been carried across the ocean by the Gulf Stream.

In deep water, the droplets of water inside a wave move around in circles.

In shallower water, the path the droplets follow is flattened and the wave builds up.

On the Crest of a Wave

Water does not move along when waves travel through it. As a wave passes, the drops of water move only up and around.

They rise towards the crest of the wave and fall as it passes. You can see this if you watch a jellyfish bobbing up and down on the sea.

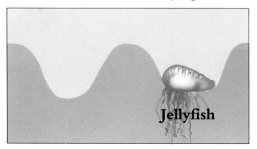

Jellyfish

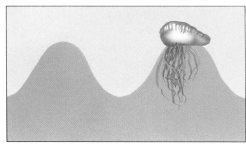

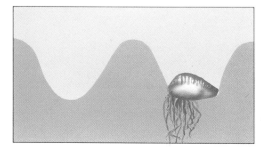

Moving Water

These are the main currents which flow through the surface of the oceans and keep the waters moving. Winds which always blow in the same direction keep the surface currents moving. But the spinning of the Earth causes currents to change direction. These currents do not affect waters below about 350 m (1,150 ft) of the surface.

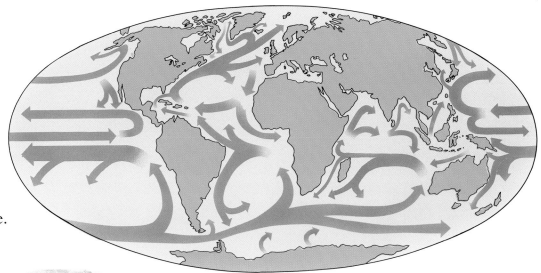

➡ **Warm Currents**
➡ **Cold Currents**

Toppling Over

When the front edge of a wave becomes too steep, the top begins to travel faster than the bottom. Eventually it topples over and "breaks". This happens in the open sea with very high waves and strong winds, but even small waves break near the shore.

Swirling Currents

Even the biggest waves do not last very long. As soon as the wind stops blowing, the waves die away and the surface of the sea may become absolutely flat. This does not mean that the sea has stopped moving. There is a complicated system of surface currents, like huge rivers in the sea, that constantly swirls the oceans.

Deep Currents

There are currents in the very deepest parts of the sea. These currents are caused by the differences in the temperature of the water. Cold water is heavier than warm water. The heaviest water sinks down from the surface in the Arctic and Antarctic oceans. It is replaced by warmer water flowing from the Tropics to the Poles.

Polar Ice

Warm Water

Cold Water

Rising and Falling

Almost everywhere in the world, the water along the shoreline does not stay in the same place all day as it does in a lake. Instead it moves up and down the beach twice every day. These movements are called tides.

The sea seems to be filling up and emptying, but it is really rising and falling with the tides. At high tide, the water piles up on to the beach. At low tide, it flows back down the beach again.

A Wide Range
The Bay of Fundy on the Atlantic coast of Canada has some of the largest tides, with a range of over 15 m (49 ft). At low tide, fishermen take fish from nets left high and dry by the outgoing tide.

Bay of Fundy

The Moon and the Sun
The tides are caused by the pull of the Sun and the Moon on the oceans. This pulling effect makes the ocean waters pile up, or bulge, on the area of the Earth that faces them. The tides rise and fall as the Earth spins on its axis and different parts of the oceans face the Moon and Sun.

High Tide Mark

Crab

Sand Hopper

Seaweed

Seaweed

Many animals live buried under the sand and mud when the tide is out.

Rock Pool

Worm Casts

Spring and Neap Tides

High and low tides do not reach the same level on the shore each day. The tidal range, the distance between the high water mark and the next low water mark, is always changing. Every two weeks there are big tides called "spring tides". These happen when the Moon and Sun pull together from the same direction. Very small "neap tides" happen when the Moon and Sun pull from different directions.

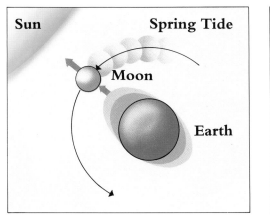

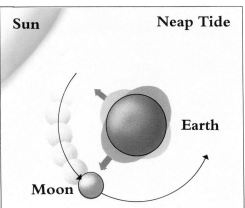

The Moon is tiny compared with the Sun, but it is so much nearer to the Earth that its effect on the tides is much greater.

Avocet

Many sea birds have long beaks to grasp animals that live under the sand.

Dead Starfish

Dead Sea Urchin

Big Tides and Little Tides

If the Earth was perfectly round like a billiard ball, and if the ocean was spread evenly all over it, the tidal range would be the same everywhere. But the odd shape of the land causes the tides to be very small in some places and very big in other places.

The Mediterranean is joined with the rest of the oceans through a narrow opening called the Strait of Gibraltar. Often called a tideless sea, it does have tides. The highest range is no more than 30 cm (1 ft) and in most places it is much less.

Tides and Harbours

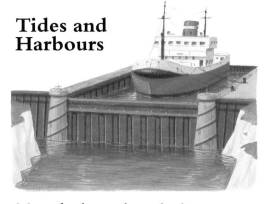

Many harbours have lock gates to keep the water in when the tide goes out, so that ships do not become stranded on the bottom.

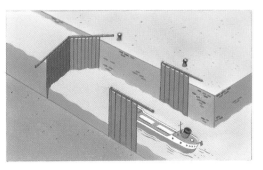

To enter a harbour, a ship passes through the gates into a short channel. The gates close and water is let in through smaller gates.

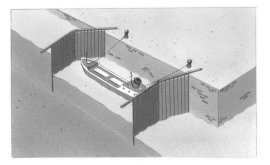

When the water level reaches the same height as the harbour water, the second set of gates opens and the ship floats into the harbour.

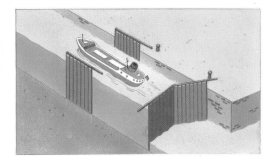

Life in the Oceans

The oceans of the world are filled with an amazing variety of life, from the warm, sunlit waters to the deep, dark trenches. Strange starfish, crabs, flying fish, angel fish, worms, turtles, sharks and huge whales all make their homes under the water.

The shape, colour and size of most sea creatures all depend on their lifestyle and where they live in the oceans. Fish that live in coral reefs are much more colourful than dull flatfish that live on the bottom and are safely camouflaged against the dark seabed.

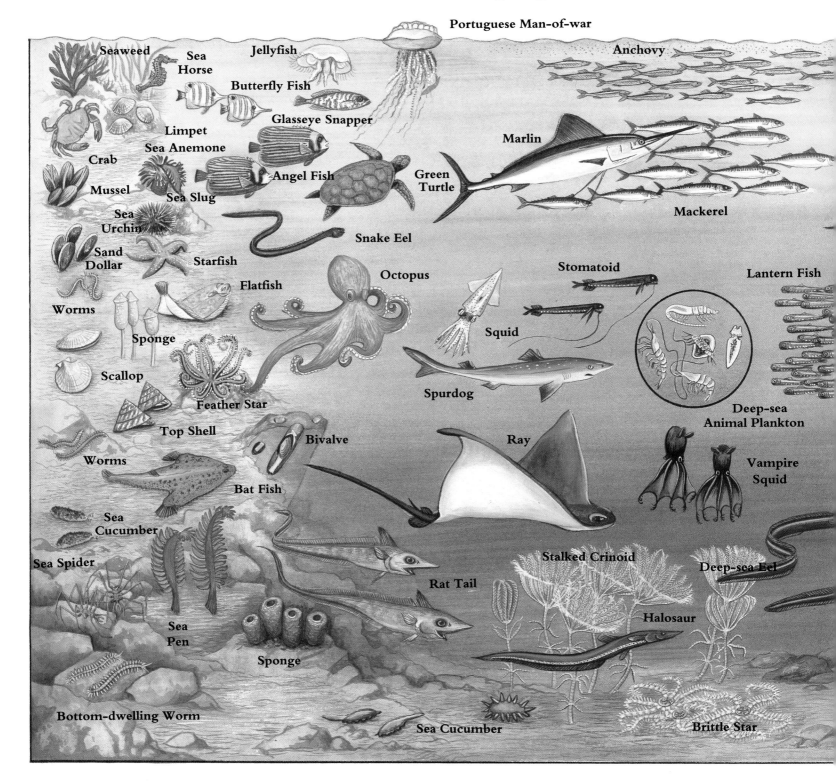

Portuguese Man-of-war
Seaweed
Sea Horse
Jellyfish
Anchovy
Butterfly Fish
Limpet
Sea Anemone
Glasseye Snapper
Marlin
Crab
Angel Fish
Green Turtle
Mussel
Sea Slug
Sea Urchin
Snake Eel
Mackerel
Sand Dollar
Starfish
Stomatoid
Lantern Fish
Worms
Flatfish
Octopus
Sponge
Squid
Scallop
Spurdog
Deep-sea Animal Plankton
Feather Star
Top Shell
Bivalve
Ray
Vampire Squid
Worms
Bat Fish
Sea Cucumber
Sea Spider
Stalked Crinoid
Deep-sea Eel
Rat Tail
Halosaur
Sea Pen
Sponge
Bottom-dwelling Worm
Sea Cucumber
Brittle Star

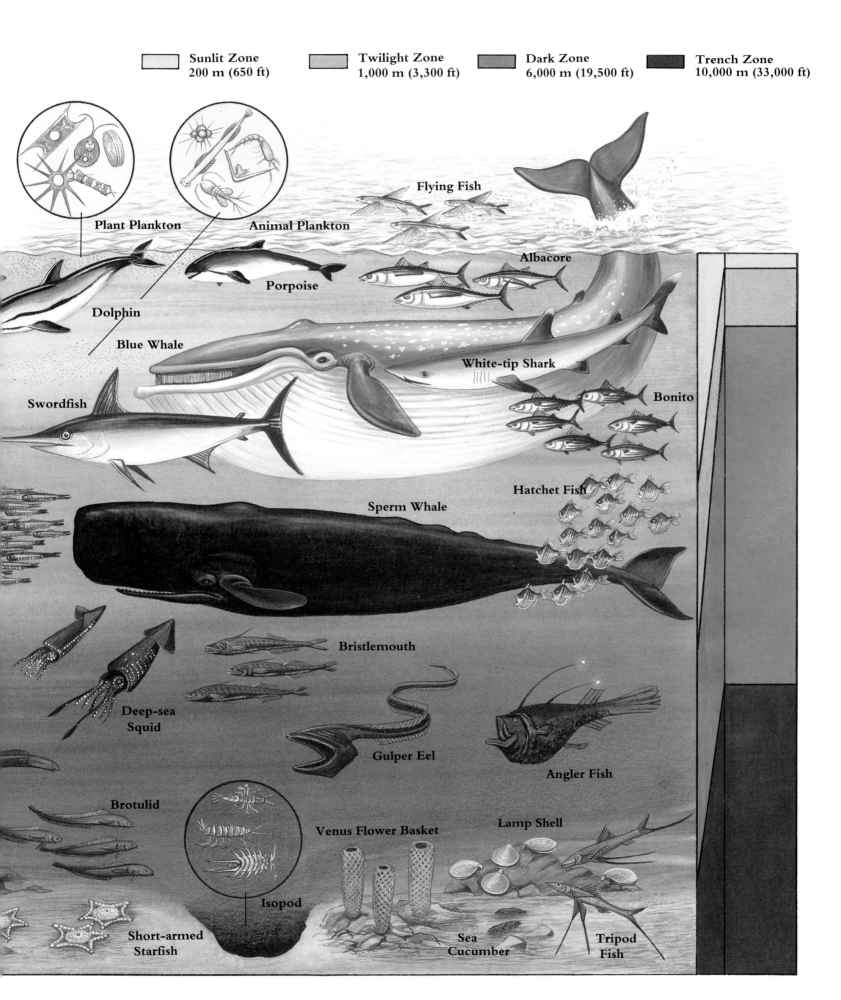

Sunlit Zone
200 m (650 ft)

Twilight Zone
1,000 m (3,300 ft)

Dark Zone
6,000 m (19,500 ft)

Trench Zone
10,000 m (33,000 ft)

Plant Plankton

Animal Plankton

Flying Fish

Albacore

Porpoise

Dolphin

Blue Whale

White-tip Shark

Swordfish

Bonito

Hatchet Fish

Sperm Whale

Bristlemouth

Deep-sea
Squid

Gulper Eel

Angler Fish

Brotulid

Lamp Shell

Venus Flower Basket

Isopod

Short-armed
Starfish

Sea
Cucumber

Tripod
Fish

Plants of the Sea

Most plants that live in the ocean belong to a group called algae. Especially adapted for life in the water, these plants, like land plants, come in many different shapes, sizes and colours. But, unlike land plants, they do not produce flowers and seeds. The best known algae are called seaweeds, found on rocky shores all over the world.

Seaweeds can grow only in shallow water, because they need sunlight to make their food. They range in size from tiny tufts a few millimetres high to giant kelps which have thick, leathery stems and long "leaves" or fronds. Huge forests of kelp can sometimes be seen floating in the water at the edge of the sea when the tide is very low.

Furbelows

Living Colour

Seaweeds can be many different colours. Some are green, like most plants, but others are red, brown or yellow. Whatever their colour, they all need sunlight to grow. A few seaweeds can live in very dim light, but none grow deeper than about 100 m (330 ft). The fixed seaweeds only grow in a narrow fringe around the continents and islands.

Sugar Kelp

Sugar kelp, a big brown seaweed, and Plocamium, a fine red seaweed, grow lower down the shore.

Serrated Wrack

Serrated wrack has fronds with sharp jagged edges.

Plocamium

Floating Plants

In the open ocean, the most important source of food for plant-eating animals are the tiny plants which float in the top layers. These floating plants, and the animals that eat them, form part of the oceans' plankton.

Plankton are all the tiny creatures that are too small or too weak to swim against the strong ocean currents. To study them, scientists collect them in very fine nets, which they pull very slowly through the water.

Plankton net open

Plankton

Plankton net closed

Thongweed

A type of seaweed called thongweed may grow over 3 m (10 ft) long.

Carragheen

Carragheen, a red seaweed, is used to make gels. Bladder wrack has big air pockets so it can stay afloat in water.

Bladder Wrack

Plant Facts

Some tiny sea plants produce poisons which can be very harmful in large quantities. These plants often turn the sea a reddish colour, causing "red tides".

The kelps of the European coasts are rarely longer than 6 m (20 ft), but giant kelps in the South Atlantic and off the coast of California reach a length of 60 m (197 ft) or more.

Roots and Leaves

Seaweeds appear to be rooted to rocks just as land plants are rooted in soil. But seaweed roots have a very different purpose. Unlike land plants, seaweeds do not take up chemicals through their roots, but get them directly from the water. The "roots", called holdfasts, anchor the plants to rocks and stop them from being washed out to sea or flung on to the shore.

Rootlets

Holdfasts and their rootlets anchor seaweeds to the sea floor. They must be strong enough to stand up to waves and currents.

Holdfasts

Tiny Jewels

Under a microscope, the plants of the plankton can be seen to form a wonderful variety of shapes and colours. Many have spines and hairs to help them stay afloat in water. Most of the plants live as separate cells, but some form long chains or balls. Small as they are, these plants are the equivalent of grass on land.

Leatherback Turtle

The Floating World

The surface of the sea is a very difficult place to live. In rough weather, creatures that live there are thrown about by the breaking waves. In calm weather, the hot Sun may dry them out, or they may fall prey to sea birds from above and fish and other enemies from below. Despite all these dangers, a few plants and animals still manage to survive on top of the water.

Floating Giants

The only time that sea turtles leave the water is when the females go ashore to lay their eggs. Males may never return to land after hatching. Turtles that feed mostly on seaweed do not stray far from the warmer coasts. Those that eat shrimps and fish sometimes wander far out into the ocean. These ocean wanderers may be carried by the strong currents far from their normal homes near the coasts.

Most turtles are about 60 cm (2 ft) long. But the largest of all, the leatherback turtle, is almost 2 m (6.6 ft) long and weighs up to half a tonne.

North America

Atlantic Ocean

Sargasso Sea

Africa

South America

Floating Weeds

When Christopher Columbus sailed across the Atlantic on his way to America, his ships were becalmed in an area in the middle of the ocean. There were no currents, hardly any wind to fill the sails, and huge masses of seaweed were found floating on the surface of the water. This area became known as the Sargasso Sea. Sailors tried to avoid it because they feared their ships would become tangled in the weed and never escape.

Sargassum Crab

Sail-by-the-wind

Sail-by-the-wind

A relative of jellyfish, a sail-by-the-wind floats on the surface of the tropical ocean. Its float is a little raft, about 7 cm (3 in) long, with a "sail" set across it from corner to corner. Inside the raft, there are chambers filled with air. They are made of a horny material similar to fingernails. These chambers last long after the animal has died and are sometimes found scattered on the shore.

A sail-by-the-wind has stinging tentacles hanging underneath its float, but they are shorter and less poisonous than a Portuguese man-of-war's.

Ianthina

Gentle Killer

A small and beautiful violet-blue snail often hangs from a sail-by-the-wind's float. The snail, which is called *Ianthina,* is not just a hitch-hiker. It actually eats all the soft parts underneath the sail-by-the-wind's raft. When it has finished, the snail floats away, hanging from a raft of slimy bubbles which it produces itself.

Portuguese Man-of-war

A Man-of-war

A Portuguese man-of-war is also a relative of jellyfish. It is found floating on the surface of the ocean in warmer parts of the world. Its gas-filled float, which grows up to 30 cm (1 ft) long, has a tall crest which acts as a sail, catching the wind as the man-of-war bobs about on the water. Brilliant blue tentacles, up to 10 m (33 ft) long, hang underneath the float.

They trail through the water like long fishing lines as the float is blown along by the wind.

The tentacles are packed with poisonous stinging cells which shoot tiny stings into anything that touches them. Large fish are often caught and paralysed by the tentacles and then pulled up to the float where a bunch of "mouths" eat them.

Sargassum Fish

The Weed Community

Many small sea creatures, including fish that disguise themselves as weeds, shelter among the Sargassum weed. Crabs and shrimps would be unable to live in the open ocean without the weed to cling to and hide in. Animals that live with the Sargassum weed rely on the gas-filled bladders of the weed to hold them up.

Toothless Pipefish

Ocean Drifters

If you pulled a fine net slowly through water close to the surface of the ocean, within a few minutes you would collect an amazing variety of tiny, beautiful sea plants and animals.

You would catch samples of almost all the main animal groups, from single-celled relatives of the amoeba to shrimps and baby fish. This is the drifting world of plankton.

Copepod

Plant Plankton

Food Chain

Tiny Ocean Plant Eaters

The plants of the plankton are so small that the animals that feed on them also have to be tiny. The most important of these are the copepods. In most places, copepods are the first vital link in the food chain. They eat the tiny plants and are in turn eaten by slightly larger animals, that are eaten by even larger ones, and so on.

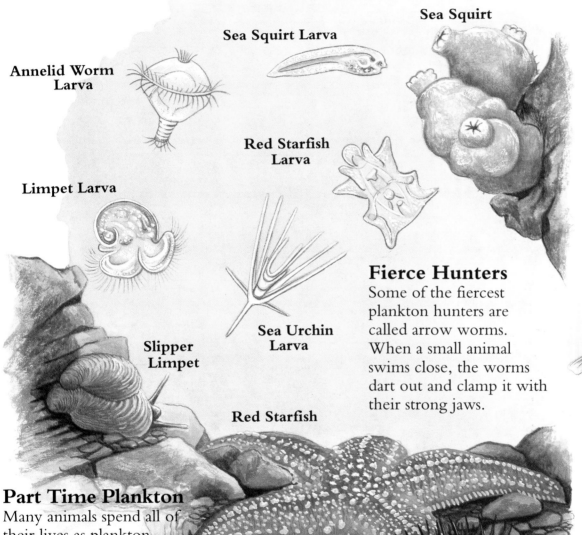

Sea Squirt Larva

Sea Squirt

Annelid Worm Larva

Red Starfish Larva

Limpet Larva

Fierce Hunters

Some of the fiercest plankton hunters are called arrow worms. When a small animal swims close, the worms dart out and clamp it with their strong jaws.

Sea Urchin Larva

Slipper Limpet

Red Starfish

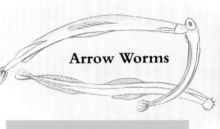

Arrow Worms

Part Time Plankton

Many animals spend all of their lives as plankton. Others begin life as plankton but move out of it when they grow bigger.

Many animals that live on the seabed as adults, such as starfish, sea urchins, worms, sea squirts and sea snails, begin life looking quite different and living in the plankton.

Annelid Worm

Sea Urchin

Ocean Facts

Hundreds of different types of copepods live in all parts of the ocean. Scientists think that there are probably more copepods in the world than all the other animals put together.

The largest jellyfish in the world is the lion's mane jellyfish. It has a bell up to 2 m (6.6 ft) across and tentacles up to 10 m (33 ft) long.

Drifting Fisherman

Some of the creatures that feed on plankton, especially many kinds of jellyfish, do not chase after their prey. They wait for their victims to bump into them.

The main part of the jellyfish, the bell, contracts and expands, like an umbrella opening and closing.

This movement is a kind of jet propulsion which drives the jellyfish slowly through the water.

Long tentacles, covered with lots of stinging cells, hang from a jellyfish's bell. When a small animal swims into them, the tentacles spear it with stings, quickly paralysing it with poison.

Cyanea

There are many different kinds of jellyfish, but they all have the same basic "umbrella" shape.

Sea Wasp

Compass Jellyfish

Rhizostoma

Pelagia

The Strange Life of a Flatfish

Flatfish that live on the seabed, such as plaice and flounder, begin life as plankton. Instead of being flat, like its parents, a baby flatfish looks quite normal, with one eye on either side of its head.

As it grows, one eye slowly moves up over the top of its head and down the other side. Eventually the young fish settles on the seabed.

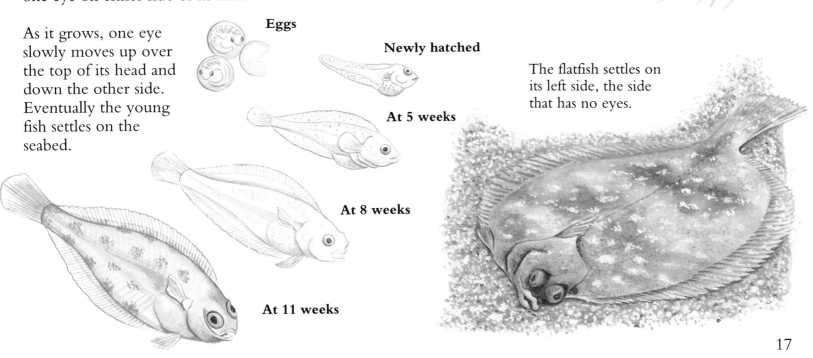

Eggs

Newly hatched

At 5 weeks

The flatfish settles on its left side, the side that has no eyes.

At 8 weeks

At 11 weeks

The World of Fish

The oceans of the world are teeming with fish, from the gigantic whale shark to the tiny dwarf pygmy goby. Over 12,000 species have already been discovered but there are probably many more kinds of fish swimming in the sea.

Fish are the most varied group of all sea creatures and come in many different shapes and sizes. But they all belong to one of two main types – "cartilaginous" or "bony" fish.

Bony Fish

All bony fish have a skeleton made of bone. Many, such as herring and cod, are shaped like a torpedo. They have a head at one end and a vertical tail fin at the other. They also have other fins, either single ones along their backs and stomachs, or paired ones along their sides. From this basic fish pattern, a huge range of strange shapes and lifestyles has developed.

Horses of the Sea

A sea horse is one of the strangest of all fish. It has a mouth at the end of its long, thin snout which it uses to snap up tiny plankton animals. A sea horse will often stop swimming and anchor itself to seaweeds and rocks with its long tail.

Unlike other fish, sea horses swim in an upright position. They drive themselves along with the help of a fin in the middle of their backs. The fin vibrates so fast that it looks like a small propeller.

Pipefish

Hidden by seaweeds, a sea horse and pipefish rest in an upright position.

Sea Horse

Herring

Snake-like Fish

Pipefish are long and thin and look a bit like snakes. Like sea horses, they often rest in an upright position. Before they mate, male and female pipefish swim past each other a few times. Eventually they link up and the male rubs the female's stomach with his snout. Then she lays her eggs in his pouch and swims away.

White-tip Shark

Cartilaginous Fish

Sharks, skates and rays have skeletons that
are not made of bone, but of a much softer
and less brittle material called cartilage.

Bony fish have a gas bladder inside their bodies
which allows them to float without swimming.
Sharks and rays do not have gas bladders, so if they
stop swimming, they sink very quickly. They live
either near the seabed, resting on the bottom, or
close to the surface, where they swim all the time.

Mako Shark

**Electric
Ray**

Sharks that Fly

Most sharks bend their
bodies and tails from side to
side as they swim. Skates and
rays are really sharks that have
become flattened from top to
bottom. Instead of using their tails,
they flap their "wings" up and down
so that they fly through the water.

Cod

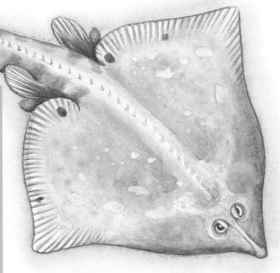

Skate

Fish Facts

The largest fish in the world is
the whale shark. It may reach a
length of more than 15 m (49 ft)
and weigh up to 15 tonnes. This
huge fish moves very slowly
and eats tiny plankton animals.

A moonfish is an unusual type
of flatfish. It has a deep, flat
body, feeds mainly on squid,
and may be as long as 3 m (10 ft).

Sea horses have a very strange
way of looking after their
young. The male has a special
pouch on his stomach where
the female lays her eggs. She
then has nothing more to do
with them. It is the male who
carries the eggs until they hatch.
He keeps the babies in his
pouch until they can live on
their own.

On the Seabed

On land, most animals move around to find food. But in the oceans, many animals that live on the dark seabed stay in the same place throughout their adult lives. They often begin life drifting in plankton before settling on the sea floor.

Many of these strange creatures look like plants. To save energy, they wait for food to float to them instead of moving around to hunt for it themselves. Many survive by feeding on dead plants and animals that fall down on them from the water far above.

Sea Pen

Crawlers

Starfish and sea urchins have hundreds of little suckers called tube feet on their undersides. These suckers all work together, sticking on to the seabed and pulling the animals along the sea floor.

Sea Urchin

Tiny Flowers

Sea pens are relatives of sea anemones and corals. They have a main stem with branches which seem to carry little flowers. But each of the "flowers" is like a tiny sea anemone. It has its own ring of dangerous tentacles to catch its prey and a mouth to eat with.

Tiny Pumps

Sponges are very simple animals that range in size from tiny mats, a few millimetres thick, to the giant loggerhead sponge of the Tropics which may be 1 m (3.3 ft) or more high. All sponges pump water through their bodies, sifting out tiny pieces of food to eat.

Sponge Skeletons

The body of a sponge is supported by a skeleton of tiny rods called spicules. The rods fit together like scaffolding.

In some sponges the spicules are very simple. In others they are quite complicated, forming beautiful shapes that look like snowflakes.

Columns of Sponge

Starfish

Chalice Sponge

Pottery Sponges

To move about, a starfish's tube feet fill with water. Each has a sucker on the end to grip the floor.

Jet-propelled

Some shellfish, such as scallops, swim by jet propulsion. They open and close their shells, forcing water out through a small, narrow opening. They can usually move only a few metres through the water before sinking back on to the sea floor.

Scallops

Good Walkers

Crabs and lobsters and their relatives are among the few sea creatures that walk along the seabed. They are called crustaceans, which means "hard-shelled".

All crustaceans have lots of legs, but crabs and lobsters have four pairs that they use especially for walking. Another pair at the front of their bodies is used for fighting and eating their food.

When they migrate, some lobsters follow each other in long lines of 60 or more.

Sea Anemones

Razor Shell

Clam

Burrowers

Where the sea floor is soft, many shellfish, such as clams and cockles, live in the soft mud to keep safe. They only poke out part of their bodies on to the seabed or into the water to collect food.

Rag Worm

American Spiny Lobsters

Crab

Poisonous Crown

Sea anemones attach themselves to a hard surface, such as a rock or a piece of shell. They have a crown of stinging tentacles which they hold up in the water. If an animal, such as a small shrimp or fish, bumps into the tentacles, it is quickly poisoned and then pulled into the anemone's mouth.

Fan Worm

Keel Worm

Marine Worms

Some marine worms hunt for food while others behave a bit like sea anemones. These worms stand upright in their tubes, which are firmly planted in the sea floor. They catch their food with tentacles spread out from the top of the tube.

1
2
3
4
5
6
7
8
9
10
11
12
13
14
15
16
17
18
19
20
21
22
23
24
25
26
27
28
29
30
31
32
33
34
35
36
37
38
39
40
41
42
43
44
45
46
47
48
49
50

Life Between the Tides

Life between the tides is not easy for the shoreline creatures. They have to stop themselves from drying out in the Sun and they must protect themselves from waves.

The higher up the shore they live, the longer they are uncovered and the tougher they have to be. On sandy and muddy shores, many creatures burrow to keep damp. On rocky shores, many cling tightly to the rocks.

Strong Weeds

Big seaweeds have thick, leathery leaves and tough stems. They are very strong and bendy so that they can stand up to the waves that crash around them. They are attached to the rocks by very strong holdfasts.

Several kinds of shore seaweed have gas-filled bladders in their leaves to help them float off the bottom when the tide is in.

Staying Still

Many seashore animals stay still when the tide is out, almost as if they are sleeping. Sea anemones pull in their tentacles and shrink their bodies into blobs. Barnacles pull their legs inside their shells and close their lids.

Under Weeds and Rocks

When the tide is out, some sea creatures shelter under big seaweeds and rocks to stay cool and damp.

Limpets

Seaweed

Crab

Starfish

Mussels clamp their two shells tightly together. At high tide, they open up and pump water into their shells to filter out food. Mussels and their relatives are called bivalves because they have two shells hinged together.

Mussels

Sea Anemones

When the tide goes out, anemones become harmless, and mussels shut their shells.

As the tide goes out, limpets always return to exactly the same spot on the seashore. Twisting their shells backwards and forwards, they scrape small hollows in the rocks which match the shape of their conical shells exactly. If the rock is very hard, the shell will be worn away to fit it. If it is soft, the rock will be worn away by the shell.

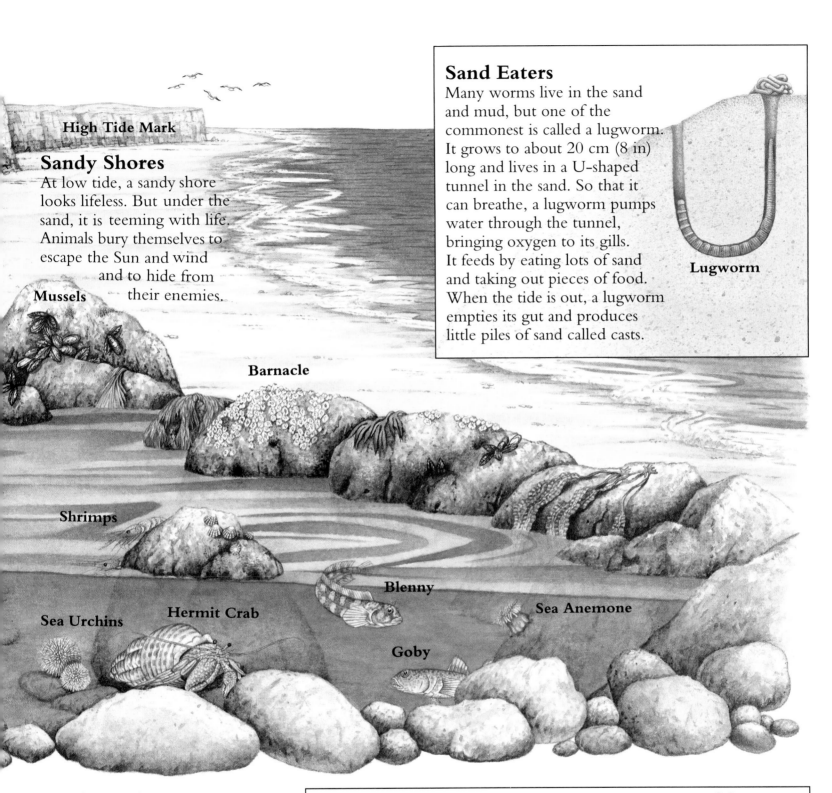

Sandy Shores

At low tide, a sandy shore looks lifeless. But under the sand, it is teeming with life. Animals bury themselves to escape the Sun and wind and to hide from their enemies.

High Tide Mark

Mussels

Barnacle

Shrimps

Sea Urchins

Hermit Crab

Blenny

Goby

Sea Anemone

Sand Eaters

Many worms live in the sand and mud, but one of the commonest is called a lugworm. It grows to about 20 cm (8 in) long and lives in a U-shaped tunnel in the sand. So that it can breathe, a lugworm pumps water through the tunnel, bringing oxygen to its gills. It feeds by eating lots of sand and taking out pieces of food. When the tide is out, a lugworm empties its gut and produces little piles of sand called casts.

Lugworm

Rock Pools

To stop themselves from drying out when the tide goes out, all sorts of seashore animals live in rock pools. Small fish, shrimps, worms, urchins, and barnacles all make their homes there. Crabs and prawns come out of their holes to hunt for food washed into the pools by the tide.

Sandhoppers

Sandhoppers, a type of shrimp, live on sandy shores. They burrow into the sand at the top of the shore, usually under dead seaweed or other rubbish thrown up by the tide.

They are called sandhoppers because they jump into the air to search for food, sometimes as high as 1 m (3.3 ft). Huge groups can often be seen jumping together.

Sandhoppers

Life in the Shallows

The part of the sea floor closest to the coasts is called the continental shelf. It never gets deeper than about 200 m (650 ft). The bottom of the shelf can be quite bumpy, with some of the bumps breaking through the surface as islands. These shelves may be hundreds of kilometres or only a few kilometres wide.

Added together, the world's continental shelves make up only about 5 per cent of the total area covered by the ocean. These shallow areas are much richer than the dark waters deeper down, and they provide us with most of the food we take from the sea.

North America   Europe
                 Asia
         Africa
South America
                 Australia

□ Continental Shelf
□ Continents

Full of Life

The continental shelves teem with animals because there is so much plant plankton for them to eat.

Rivers carry chemical fertilizers from the land. Plant plankton use them to grow and multiply.

Swimming in Shoals

Herrings live in mid-water where they feed on tiny plankton animals. They swim together in huge shoals, or groups, moving up and down in the water as they hunt their prey.

Herring

Seasons in the Sea

In tropical shallow waters, plants grow at the same rate all year around. In colder areas, far from the Equator, there are seasons in the sea.

In these areas, there is more plant plankton in the Spring and Summer. To take advantage of these plants, the animal plankton breed then.

Spring

Summer

Autumn

Winter

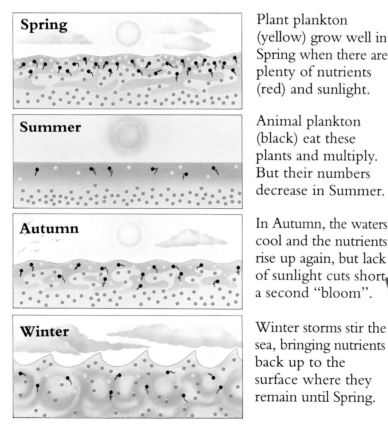

Plant plankton (yellow) grow well in Spring when there are plenty of nutrients (red) and sunlight.

Animal plankton (black) eat these plants and multiply. But their numbers decrease in Summer.

In Autumn, the waters cool and the nutrients rise up again, but lack of sunlight cuts short a second "bloom".

Winter storms stir the sea, bringing nutrients back up to the surface where they remain until Spring.

Tuna and their relatives can travel great distances. North American bluefins travel across the Atlantic to Europe.

Mackerel

Bluefin Tuna

The Best Swimmers

Mackerels and their relatives are the best swimmers of all. Some of the smaller species spend most of their time over the continental shelves, eating plankton and small fish. Larger fish, such as tuna, travel hundreds or thousands of kilometres across the open ocean in search of food.

Giant Crabs

There are more than 4,500 different kinds of crabs in the sea. They range from tiny ones, just a few millimetres wide, to the giant Japanese spider crab which may be almost 3 m (10 ft) from claw to claw.

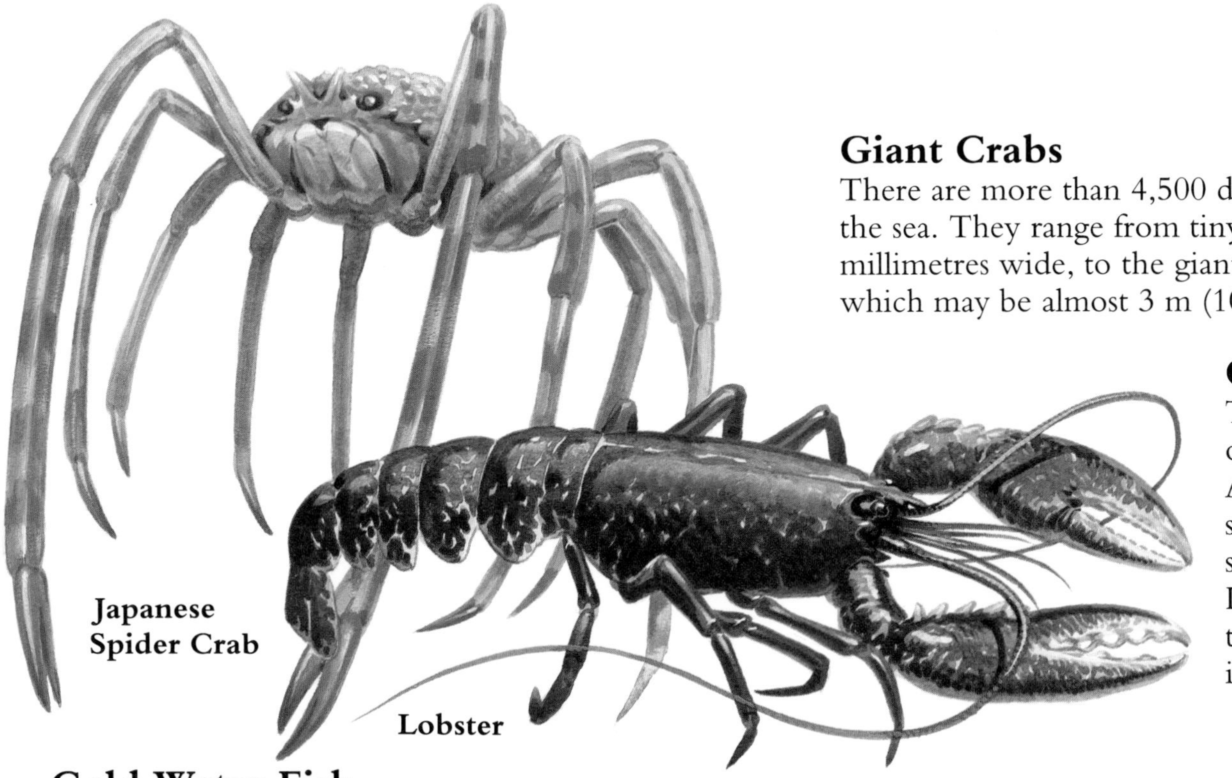

Great Claws

The "common" lobster of Europe and North America lives in cold, shallow water and usually shelters in rock crevices. It uses its great claws to crush and tear apart its food.

Japanese Spider Crab

Lobster

Cold Water Fish

Cod, hake, haddock and whiting are all cold-water fish. They spend most of their time close to the seabed where they feed on other fish. There are similar species of cold-water fish in both the southern and northern halves of the world. Many swim great distances to find food, but they all return to special breeding places.

Cod

Haddock

Hake

Whiting

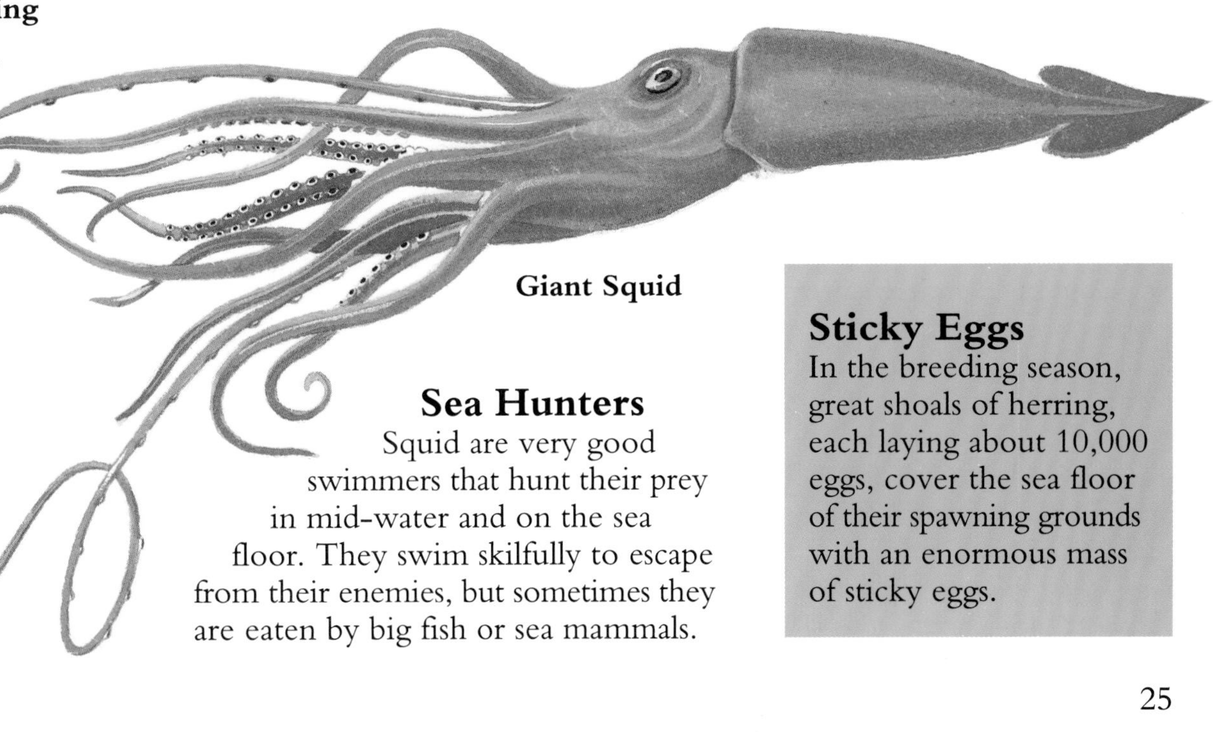

Giant Squid

Squid can move very quickly. Their streamlined bodies fill with water and then contract, sending out a powerful stream of water.

Sea Hunters

Squid are very good swimmers that hunt their prey in mid-water and on the sea floor. They swim skilfully to escape from their enemies, but sometimes they are eaten by big fish or sea mammals.

Sticky Eggs

In the breeding season, great shoals of herring, each laying about 10,000 eggs, cover the sea floor of their spawning grounds with an enormous mass of sticky eggs.

The Twilight Zone

If you were to walk across the continental shelf from the shore towards the middle of the ocean, you would eventually reach an area where the seabed begins to slope more steeply towards the great depths. You would then be at the top of the continental slope, the true "edge" of the continent.

As you move down the slope, the light becomes dimmer until there is no light from above. The area between the light surface waters and the deep dark sea is called the twilight zone. Some of the most fantastic sea creatures of all have adapted to life in this strange murky world.

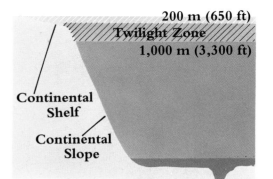

200 m (650 ft)
Twilight Zone
1,000 m (3,300 ft)

Continental Shelf

Continental Slope

Animal Camouflage

Animals that live in the twilight zone are coloured to blend in with their surroundings to help them hide from their enemies and their prey. Those living a few metres below the surface are often blue to blend in with the bright blue background of that part of the sea.

Further down in the twilight zone, many animals of the plankton become transparent, so that light passes through them and they become almost invisible.

Most deep-sea shrimps are a brilliant red colour. The light in the sea at these depths is completely blue, which makes red a very difficult colour to see. As black is also hard to see, many fish are black.

Copepod

Luminous Prawn

Luminous prawns and krill are both crustaceans which are able to produce light.

Transparent copepods swim in the plankton without being seen.

Krill

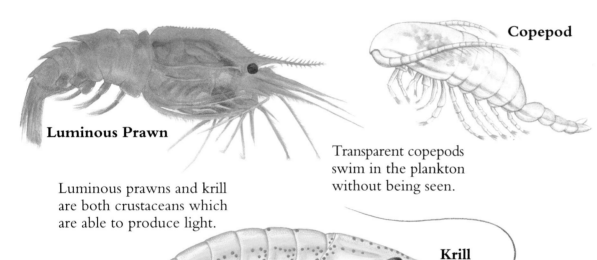

Little Light Bulbs

A shrimp or fish in the twilight zone would be easy to see from below. They would stand out as dark shapes against a dim background. So many of them have a row of organs along their underside that produce light, like little light bulbs, to make themselves invisible.

They are able to change the colour and the strength of the lights to match their surroundings. In this way, they stay invisible as they move up and down in the sea.

Great Swallower

Great swallowers have big, stretchy stomachs. Lantern fish can be identified by the pattern of their light organs.

Lantern Fish

Living Lights

Many animals produce their own living light in the sea. This is known as bioluminescence. As well as helping to camouflage them, some creatures use the lights as a signalling system. The lights help them both to recognize each other in the dark water and to attract mates. For others, the lights are used to frighten off predators or to help them hunt.

Silvery Scales

A hatchet fish is tiny, only about 3 cm (1.2 in) long. Its body is so flat that it looks very narrow from below. The sides of its body are covered with silvery scales, like tiny mirrors, which reflect the light. It also has amazing light organs that match the colour and strength of the light in the water.

1 Risso's
  Lantern Fish
2 Viper Fish
3 Hatchet Fish
4 Angler Fish
5 Flashlight Fish

Invisible Hunter

Some deep-sea fish have special lights on their heads to light up their prey. Most bioluminescence in the sea, like the incoming sunlight, is blue. If this light shines on a red shrimp, the fish still cannot see it.

Flashlight fish have red filters across their light organs, and eyes that are sensitive to red light. They can see their prey quite easily without being seen themselves.

Dangerous Lights

Deep-sea angler fish use light to lure their prey. They have a long, thin "rod" growing from the top of their heads. At the end of the rod is a small light organ that dangles over the fish's mouth. Any curious shrimp or smaller fish attracted to the light is quickly snapped up. Many angler fish have big jaws and needle-sharp teeth.

But they are usually no more than a few centimetres long, making them dangerous only to tiny animals.

Angler Fish

Down in the Depths

In the middle of the nineteenth century, when scientists began to study the deep ocean, it was thought that no life existed below a few hundred metres. Now we know that animals inhabit the whole of the oceans, down to the bottoms of the deep-sea trenches, over 11,000 m (36,200 ft) deep.

Fewer animals are able to survive in the dark, deep waters because it is much harder for them to find food. Finding enough food without using too much energy is very important for many deep-sea animals. Instead of hunting for something to eat, many lie in wait for food to come to them.

Continental Shelf

Continental Slope

1,000 m (3,300 ft)

Dark Zone

6,000 m (19,500 ft)

Three-legged Fish

Tripod fish have very long rays on the fins at the front of their bodies and also on their tail fin. They use these rays like legs to support themselves on the sea floor. They then sit and wait for food to come their way instead of swimming to find it. These strange fish are all hermaphrodite, that is they are both male and female at the same time. They are probably hermaphrodite because it is so hard for them to find a mate so deep down in the sea.

Tripod Fish

Mouths on Stalks

Lots of different kinds of deep-sea animals have long stalks to hold them high above the sea floor. They use the stalks to catch tiny food particles swept along by currents on the seabed. Stalked starfish, called feather stars, have a ring of arms around their mouths. They are raised on the end of a long stalk, firmly planted in the seabed.

Sea Lily

Feather Star

Sea Cucumbers

A Deep Sea Feast

Most of the food which floats down to the deep sea from the layers above comes in tiny pieces. But sometimes much larger pieces, including the bodies of large fish and whales, also sink to the deep ocean floor. A special community of scavengers waits for these feasts.

Deep Sea Scavengers

The first scavengers to arrive at a carcass are usually small shrimps. These tiny animals attack in such large numbers that a large fish becomes a bare skeleton within a day or two.

Within an hour or two, scavenging fish arrive to join in the feast, followed by lots of other fish. They are probably attracted to the carcass by the smell carried by the currents.

Scavenging Shrimps

Late Lunch

Scavengers that move very slowly, such as snails, reach the carcass much later. They eat tiny pieces of food left by the others. In a few days there will be nothing left but the skeleton. Even this will be broken down by bacteria.

Living "Hoovers"

Sea cucumbers of all shapes, colours and sizes crawl slowly over the sea floor hoovering up the mud for food. Some have large "tails" growing from their bodies. These may keep the cucumbers from sinking into the soft mud on the seabed.

Deep-sea Fish

Snail

Sea Urchins

Circling Worms

Some burrowing worms that are just a few centimetres long in shallow waters grow to 1 m (3.3 ft) or more in the deep sea. They live in holes on the seabed, but spread their long bodies over the soft mud in search of food, leaving behind big circle marks.

Burrowing Worm

Colourful Coral Reefs

Beautiful and brilliantly coloured coral reefs grow in warmer parts of the world, where there is plenty of sunlight. The biggest living structures on Earth, they provide hunting grounds and hiding places for all kinds of strange sea creatures. Coral reefs are found in the Red Sea, around the islands of the Pacific and Indian Oceans, in the East and West Indies and in the Caribbean. The largest of all is the Great Barrier Reef off northeastern Australia. This reef is about 2,000 km (1,250 miles) long.

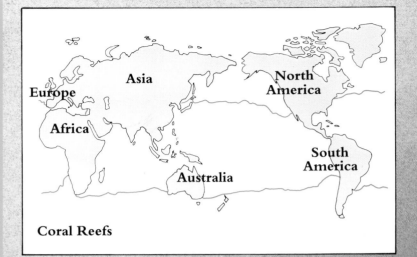

Coral Reefs

Coral reefs grow only in the tropical oceans, where the sea temperature does not fall below 20°C (68°F).

Tiny Builders

The reef itself is built by masses of tiny flower-like animals related to sea anemones. Each little "flower", called a polyp, sits in a tiny cup of hard, chalky material. Hundreds or thousands of polyps are joined together to form a single coral "colony".

Although the coral reef may be huge, only the surface layer has living coral. The deeper layers are made of the remains of long-dead corals.

Little Partners

Inside the tissues of each polyp, there are hundreds of tiny plants very similar to the algae that float in the plankton. The coral and algae live together in a partnership which is useful to both. Because algae need sunlight to grow, living coral reefs can only exist in sunlit, shallow waters.

Shapes and Patterns

Each coral species grows in a different shape. Some form great rounded masses with complicated patterns on the surface. Others, such as tube corals, grow thin branches like trees or bushes.

The combination of shapes makes the reef a wonderfully complicated structure. Miniature mountains, caves, valleys and tunnels provide shelter for animals living in and around the reef.

Parrot Fish

Red Sea Whips

Blue Coral

Bubble Coral

Platform Coral

Mushroom Coral

Colonial Coral

Giant Clam

Brain Coral

Sea Fan

Butterfly Fish

Puffer Fish

Sea Anemone

Boxfish

Sponge

Starfish

Snakelocks Anemone

Cone Shells

Moray Eel

Parrot Fish

Many fish have special features to help them feed among the crowded reefs. Parrot fish have mouths like beaks and strong jaws so that they can eat coral. They break off pieces of coral, chew them up and spit out the useless shell.

Balloon Fish

Puffer fish look quite normal until they are alarmed. If attacked, they fill themselves with water and blow up like balloons, with sharp spines sticking out all over. This defence works against most predators.

"Cowfish"

Trunkfish are protected from the sharp coral by a hard, bony case around their bodies. They are sometimes called cowfish because some have bony "horns" on their heads.

Among the Corals

Great shoals of colourful fish swim among and around the coral reefs. Of the 10,000 fish species known to live in shallow water, over half live in the reefs. These fish need to be very agile to move and feed among the corals. Many swim a kind of breast stroke with their paired fins. They use their tail fins to steer.

Colourful Community

As well as the thousands of species of fish on a coral reef, there are many other strange creatures, such as sponges, anemones, worms and shellfish.

Beautiful but Dangerous

Cone shells can be very dangerous to people. The animals inside these shells can give an extremely poisonous bite which may paralyse and kill a person.

The giant clam of the Australian Barrier Reef is the largest mollusc. It grows to a length of 1 m (3.3 ft). It is not really dangerous, but there are stories of swimmers being drowned after getting their legs caught in a shell that has snapped shut.

The fierce moray eel lurks in crevices in the coral, ready to dart out and snap up almost anything that crosses its path.

Under the Ice

The waters of the Arctic and Antarctic are freezing cold but they are teeming with life. For hundreds of years, people have hunted fish, seals and whales in the polar seas.

Although they are both huge icy wastes, the Arctic and Antarctic are quite different from each other. The Arctic is mainly ocean surrounded by land, while the Antarctic is land surrounded by ocean.

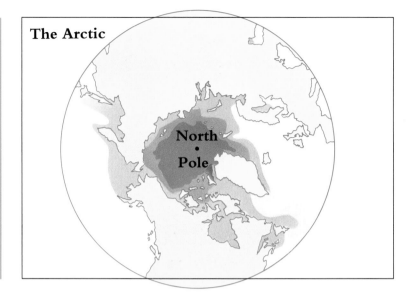

The Arctic

North Pole

This map shows the chilly ocean, surrounded by land-masses and many islands, within the Arctic Circle.

The Arctic World

The North Pole is in the middle of the Arctic Ocean. Surrounding this ocean are the landmasses of northern America, northern Europe, Asia and Greenland. Underneath the ice at the North Pole, which is about 3 m (10 ft) thick, there are hundreds of metres of open water.

The Antarctic World

The ice at the South Pole rests on a huge landmass, the Antarctic continent, which is surrounded by the southern parts of the Atlantic, Indian and Pacific oceans. These chilly waters are called the Southern Ocean. The ice covers the ocean like a big crust.

From time to time, pieces of ice may break off from its edge to form huge icebergs, sometimes tens of kilometres long. They are usually much bigger than icebergs in the Arctic.

Arctic Seals

The most common Arctic seal is the small ringed seal which grows to about 1.5 m (5 ft). It is found wherever there is open water and may even reach the North Pole itself. Like all mammals, the ringed seal has to breathe air. It finds holes in the ice where it can come up to breathe. Eskimos and polar bears wait by these holes to catch the seals as they surface.

Colony of Ringed Seals

Polar Bear

Ringed Seal

Walrus

Walruses live in the Arctic waters. Males may be 3.5 m (11 ft) long and weigh over 1.5 tonnes. They use their tusks, which grow up to 1 m (3.3 ft) long, to dig up clams and mussels.

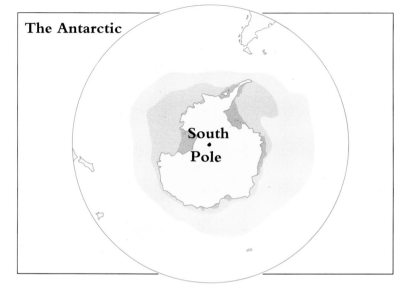

The Antarctic

South Pole

This map shows the frozen land and cold water that lie within the Antarctic Circle.

Polar Plants

The tiny plants of the plankton grow very well in the polar seas. This is because lots of fertilizing chemicals are carried there by currents from deeper water and are stirred up by the storms. Some of these plants actually live and grow in the ice itself.

Little Links

In the Antarctic Ocean, the most important of the animal plankton are krill, small shrimps about 5 cm (2 in) long. They eat plants and are in turn eaten by fish, seals and whales.

Antarctic Seals

There are four types of seals which live in and around the Antarctic ice. The most common is the crab-eater seal, which is about 2 m (6.6 ft) long. Despite its name, it feeds on krill. The Weddell seal and the Ross seal are slightly larger and eat fish and squid. The largest Antarctic seal, at 3 m (10 ft) long, is the leopard seal. It eats penguins and other large prey.

The Elephant Seal

The biggest seals of all, elephant seals, live on the edge of the Southern Ocean. Adult males may be 6 m (20 ft) long and weigh more than 3 tonnes. They have big inflatable bags on their noses that can fill up with air and blood to impress females and frighten their rival males.

Keeping Warm

Water temperatures in the Arctic and Antarctic fall as low as -2°C (29°F). Seals and whales have a thick layer of fat, called blubber, under their skin to help them keep warm. The fatty blubber acts as an insulator, keeping their body temperature much higher than the temperature of the freezing sea.

The fish of the polar oceans have special chemicals in their blood. These chemicals act just like the antifreeze we put into car radiators to stop them from freezing.

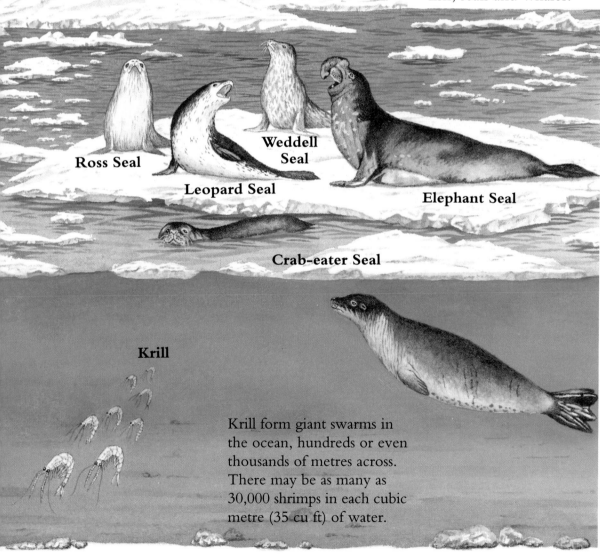

Ross Seal

Leopard Seal

Weddell Seal

Elephant Seal

Crab-eater Seal

Krill

Krill form giant swarms in the ocean, hundreds or even thousands of metres across. There may be as many as 30,000 shrimps in each cubic metre (35 cu ft) of water.

Hot Water Springs

In recent years, scientists have discovered strange creatures that cluster around hot water springs on the dark seabed. In the oceans, there are mountainous ridges along which molten rocks burst through the sea floor to form a new section of seabed. In some places, seawater passes through parts of the new seabed and gets heated by the hot rocks.

The water then rushes back into the sea as a hot water vent. These vents have been found mostly between depths of 2,500 to 3,000 m (8,200 to 9,900 ft). The pressure there is so great that the water can be heated to 300°C (572°F) or more without boiling. The water is also full of chemicals that special bacteria use for energy, just as green plants use sunlight.

In Hot Water

Bacteria that live in the vents have to be able to withstand the very high temperatures that would kill most creatures. But only a metre or two away from the vents, the temperature falls to about 2°C (36°F). The animals around the vents do not have to live in the boiling hot water.

Easy Meals

Animals living on the seabed and fish swimming close by are attracted to deep-sea vents because they can easily find food. Strange animals that are not found anywhere else, such as giant worms and blind crabs, live around the vents. Almost 200 vent animals have been discovered.

Giant Clams

Giant white clams up to 30 cm (1 ft) wide live in some of the hot water vents. Bacteria living inside their large shells provide the clams with the food they need.

Fish

Giant Clam

Sea Anemone

Eyes that "See" Heat

Some of the vents found in the Atlantic have huge populations of special shrimps that feed on bacteria growing in and near the hot water springs. The shrimps' eyes cannot see light, but they can sense the invisible radiation produced by the hot water.

Shrimp

Giant Worms

One of the most amazing of all vent animals are the enormous tube worms, which may grow to almost 2 m (6.6 ft) long. Their bright red bodies at the top of long white tubes make them look like big bunches of flowers. These worms feed by absorbing chemicals through their gills. Bacteria inside their tissues turn the chemicals into food.

Tube Worm

Dangerous "Smokers"

In some vents, the hot water is so full of chemicals that it rises from the sea floor like black smoke. As the hot water cools, the chemicals settle on the sea floor, forming tubes that look like tiny chimneys. They get taller and taller until they become wobbly and fall over.

The sides of these chimneys are very dangerous places. An animal living here always risks being boiled if the chimney breaks and releases the hot water inside. The large amounts of bacteria growing here make the risk worthwhile. Some worms crawl to the very edge of the chimneys to eat the bacteria. But they may pay for it with their lives.

Crab

Black Smoker

Sea Anemone

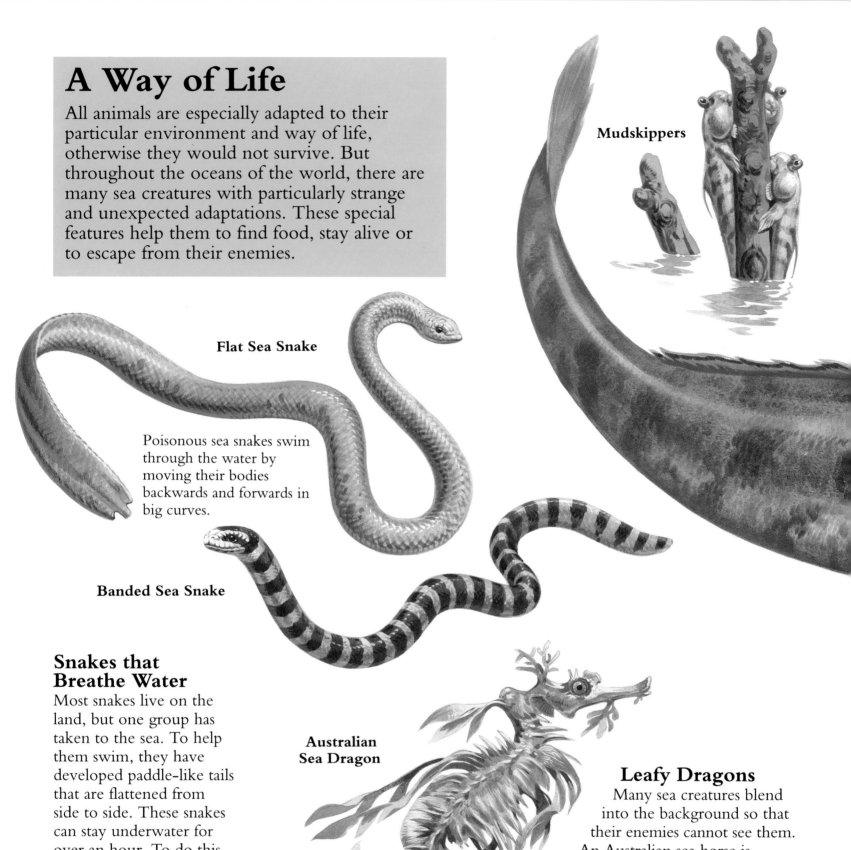

A Way of Life

All animals are especially adapted to their particular environment and way of life, otherwise they would not survive. But throughout the oceans of the world, there are many sea creatures with particularly strange and unexpected adaptations. These special features help them to find food, stay alive or to escape from their enemies.

Mudskippers

Flat Sea Snake

Poisonous sea snakes swim through the water by moving their bodies backwards and forwards in big curves.

Banded Sea Snake

Snakes that Breathe Water

Most snakes live on the land, but one group has taken to the sea. To help them swim, they have developed paddle-like tails that are flattened from side to side. These snakes can stay underwater for over an hour. To do this, they keep swallowing and spitting out water as if they are breathing. They take the oxygen they need from the water, just like fish.

Australian Sea Dragon

Leafy Dragons

Many sea creatures blend into the background so that their enemies cannot see them. An Australian sea horse is especially good at camouflaging itself. This delicate sea dragon is one of the biggest sea horses and may grow over 30 cm (1 ft) long. It has long, leafy flaps of skin on its body to help it hide among the seaweed in which it lives.

Mudskippers have a thick layer of skin around their eyes to protect them. To attract a mate, male mudskippers raise their stubby fins.

Tiny Mates

One of the biggest problems for animals in the deep ocean is finding a mate. Some female angler fish have solved this problem by carrying their husbands with them. In this species, the males are much smaller than the females. Early in a male's life, it finds a female and bites on to her skin. Now the male no longer feeds for himself but gets food from the female's body. In return, he will fertilize her eggs when they are ready.

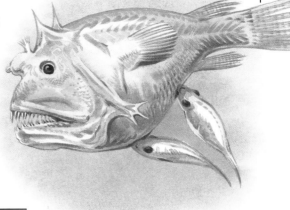

Female Angler Fish with two males

Fish that Breathe Air

Several freshwater fish breathe air and some of them have developed lungs in addition to their gills. Breathing air is very rare in the sea, but some odd fish, called mudskippers, have become very good at it and can survive out of water for several hours. They skip across the mud on their short, stubby fins and sometimes climb trees to eat insects. Like frogs, mudskippers can breathe air through their skin. They survive on land mainly by keeping their gills tightly shut so that they do not lose water and dry out. Otherwise they would suffocate in air.

Mudskipper

Oily Sharks

Most sharks are very heavy and have to keep swimming to stay afloat. But one group of sharks, called squaloid sharks, that live at the bottom of the deep sea have found another way of surviving. To help them stay afloat, they store oil in their livers because oil is lighter than water. The liver in most animals, including human beings, is no more than about 5 per cent of their total body weight.

But a squaloid shark's liver weighs about 25 per cent of its total weight. Its liver is so big that it makes the shark look quite fat compared with its sleek and slender relatives.

Squaloid Shark

Special Defences

When they are attacked by an enemy, most animals in the sea try to escape. They may get away by simply swimming faster than their attacker.

Others escape by reaching the safety of a hole or a burrow. But some have developed some amazing tricks to stay alive and escape from predators.

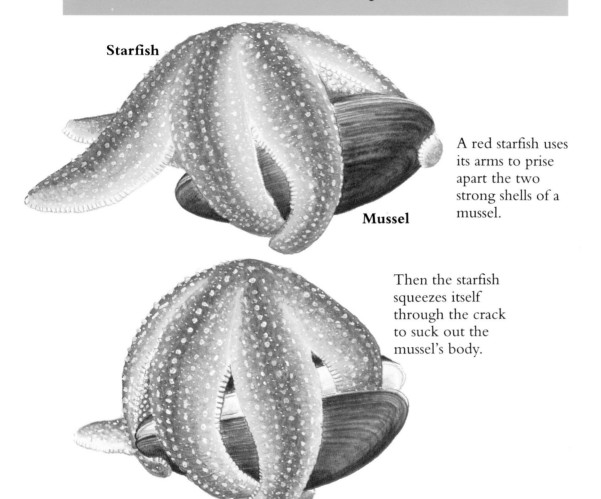

Starfish

Mussel

A red starfish uses its arms to prise apart the two strong shells of a mussel.

Then the starfish squeezes itself through the crack to suck out the mussel's body.

Sticky Threads

Sea cucumbers are relatives of starfish and sea urchins. When threatened, they shoot out a mass of sticky, poisonous threads from their mouths to frighten off hungry predators. These sticky threads grow back in a few weeks.

A European cotton-spinner has special glands which produce a sticky substance. When it is mixed with seawater, it forms a mass of sticky threads. If attacked, the cotton-spinner shoots out this substance, covering its enemy in a sticky mess.

Shell Shock

Mussels, oysters and their relatives have two strong bony shells which are hinged together. When they eat, they open the shells, uncovering their soft bodies inside. As soon as a mussel senses an enemy, it snaps its shells together and holds them shut with a very powerful muscle.

Some enemies have developed ways of opening the shells. Sea gulls carry mussels high in the air and drop them on to rocks to break them open. Starfish pull on a mussel's shells with the suckers on their arms. The mussel becomes so tired that it cannot hold its shells shut.

A dog whelk sits on a mussel and bores a hole into the shell with its tongue. When the hole is big enough, the whelk pushes its tongue through and licks out the mussel.

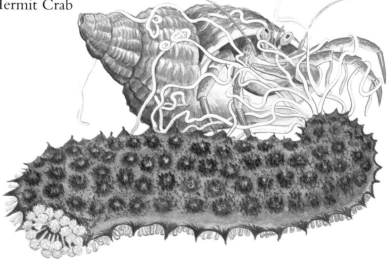

Sea Cucumber trapping Hermit Crab

Sea Slug

Borrowed Stingers

Sea slugs have bunches of frilly lobes growing out of their bodies. They are often brightly coloured to warn other animals that they are not good to eat. Sea slugs mostly eat sea anemones, cleverly storing the stings of their prey in the lobes of their bodies. If an animal tries to eat the slug, it may poison its attacker with its "borrowed" stings.

A sea slug can swallow a sea anemone without being poisoned by its stinging tentacles.

Sea Slug

This brightly coloured slug has no true gills. Instead, it breathes through the tentacles that cover its back.

Sea Slug eating
Sea Anemone

Pistol Packing Shrimp

One type of shrimp, called a pistol shrimp or snapping shrimp, can make a very loud noise, just like a gunshot. It makes the noise with a special claw. The part that moves, called the finger, has a catch at its base like the trigger on a gun. A big muscle inside the claw pulls the finger harder and harder until the trigger suddenly releases. The finger snaps shut, making a loud noise. A pistol shrimp uses its noise to frighten enemies and stun its prey.

Pistol Shrimp

Electric Shockers

Electric rays are usually small, slow moving fish that spend most of their time resting on the seabed. The largest electric ray, the torpedo, grows to 2 m (6.6 ft) and is common in European waters.

Electric rays have muscles which act as batteries in their bodies and can give a powerful shock. They use the shocks to protect themselves against enemies and stun prey. A torpedo's shock can stun a person.

Electric Nerves

Electric Organ

Electric Ray

Perfect Partners

Many sea creatures live with other animals in a partnership which helps them both. Sometimes the animals cannot survive without each other, but more often, their strange partnerships are not necessary. Each partner can survive alone, but they find life easier if they live together. Often, it is obvious how one animal benefits, but not so clear whether the other does or not.

Shark

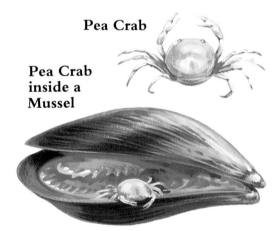

Shark Partners

Small pilot fish swim beside sharks and eat what the shark leaves behind. It was once thought that the pilot fish guided the shark to food. But the shark probably gains nothing from the partnership. No one knows why the shark does not eat the pilot fish.

Special Service

Many warm-water shrimps offer a cleaning service to the local fish. Perched on sea anemones or corals, these brightly coloured shrimps wave their claws and feelers to attract customers.

Fish swim close to the shrimps and stay quite still. The shrimps then crawl over the fish, removing parasites from their skin. Some fish open their mouths to let the shrimps clean their gills.

Cleaner Shrimp and Fish

Pea Crab

Pea Crab inside a Mussel

The Pea Crab's Home

Pea crabs are small crabs that do not grow hard shells. Instead, they live inside the shells of mussels, oysters or cockles where they steal tiny bits of food from their host.

Sometimes a female pea crab grows too big and cannot leave the host's shell. To mate, the smaller male visits the female in her prison. The host does not seem to benefit from this strange partnership at all.

Boxing Anemones

Two small crabs from the Indian and the Pacific oceans carry tiny anemones on their claws. The crabs look as if they are wearing boxing gloves. They push the anemones with their stinging tentacles towards any would-be attacker.

Crab with Sea Anemones

If something happens to their shark, the pilot fish swim around it in a frenzy before finding a new partner.

Remora

Taken for a Ride

Many shrimps and crabs live on top of other animals, particularly sea urchins and their relatives. This not only gives them a free lift, but also enables them to hide among their partner's prickly spines. It is not clear what the sea urchin gains from this partnership. Perhaps the crab or shrimp cleans the urchin's skin, like the cleaner shrimps.

Sea Urchin and Shrimps

Mobile Homes

Hermit crabs do not have shells of their own. Instead they live in empty snail shells. Some hermit crabs stick a sea anemone on to their shells. The stinging tentacles of the anemone help to protect the crab from predators. In return, the sea anemone feeds on tiny scraps of food left over by the crab.

Pilot Fish

When the hermit grows too big for its shell, it finds a bigger one. It sticks the anemone on to its new shell.

Hitch–hikers of the Sea

Strange fish called remoras have a special fin, like a big flat sucker, on top of their heads. They use it to stick on to sharks and other big fish. Then they eat the fish's leftovers. In some places, fishermen tie a line around a remora's tail and throw it into the sea near a turtle. When a remora attaches itself to the turtle they pull both in.

Sometimes the hermit and anemone have a third partner. A worm may live deep in the hermit's shell. The worm pokes its head out of the shell when the crab is eating and steals scraps of food to eat.

Sea Anemone

A threatened hermit crab hides in its shell, using its claw to block the entrance.

Hermit Crab

A Sea of Sharks

Most people think of sharks as fierce killers with fins that slice through the water towards a helpless victim. Although there are a few types of sharks that may attack and kill people, most are harmless. Many sharks are powerful swimmers with streamlined bodies. Some have huge jaws with rows of razor-sharp, triangular teeth.

Biggest and Smallest

There are more than 250 species of sharks living in the sea. They range in size from the tiny dwarf Pacific shark, which is only about 10 cm (4 in) long, to the huge whale shark, which is nearly 15 m (49 ft) long and weighs about 15 tonnes.

Harmless Giants

The enormous whale shark has tiny teeth and feeds on small plankton animals. It lives in the warmer parts of the oceans, swimming slowly near the surface with its huge mouth wide open. Plankton is filtered from the water as it passes out of the whale shark's gills. Basking sharks live in the cooler areas of the ocean, and may grow longer than 12 m (39 ft). Like whale sharks, they eat animal plankton and are harmless to humans.

Basking Shark

Dogfish

Tough Tail

A thresher shark gets its name from its long, tough tail which bends up and down like a whip. It swims around and around big shoals of herring or mackerel, thrashing the water with its tail. This forces the fish into a small area where the shark then devours them.

Thresher Shark

Whale Shark

A whale shark is the biggest fish, but a great white shark is the most dangerous. Every year it attacks many swimmers.

Slow Movers

Many sharks move very slowly. They eat shrimps, crabs, snails and worms. Nurse sharks and dogfish are only about 3 m (10 ft) long. They are not very streamlined and live near the seabed where they can find food.

The Jagged Edge

One of the most feared sharks is the great white shark. It grows to about 10 m (33 ft), and has a set of sharp, triangular teeth with jagged edges. These teeth are perfect for stabbing and tearing apart the flesh of its victims.

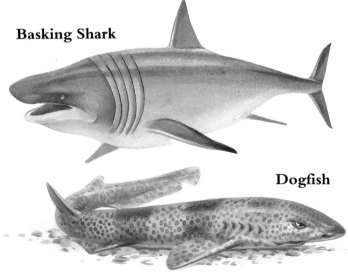

Slashing Teeth

Blue sharks and tiger sharks are smaller than great white sharks. They usually grow to about 5 m (16 ft).

Like a great white, they have sharp, slashing teeth and can swim very quickly, but only over short distances.

Tiger Shark

Blue Shark

Shark Attack

Only about ten species of sharks are known to attack people. The fiercest and most active live in mid-water, where they hunt fish and other large prey. They are streamlined and slender and can swim very fast.

Hunting by Smell

Most sharks can smell their prey. They can smell blood at great distances in the sea. Spear fishermen may find sharks swimming towards them very soon after they have speared a fish. Sometimes the sharks attack the fishermen as they try to steal the fish.

Heads Like Hammers

One of the strangest-looking sharks is the hammerhead shark. Its head is shaped like a huge hammer with one eye on either side. This may give it better eyesight for hunting fish. Sometimes hammerheads attack and kill people.

Hammerhead Shark

Great White Shark

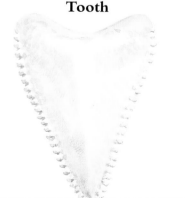

Great White Shark Tooth

This vicious shark lives in warmer parts of the sea.

A great white shark's tooth is about 8 cm (3 in) long. But fossil teeth more than twice as big have been found. They probably belonged to huge animals at least 30 m (98 ft) long.

Working Together

Most sharks hunt alone, but sand sharks, which live off the Atlantic coast of North America, hunt in large shoals. They drive their victims into a tight bunch in shallow water, and then rush in and seize them.

Sand Shark

Incredible Journeys

Many animals in the sea make regular journeys to find food or to breed. These special journeys are repeated by the same species time after time. This travelling is called migration. It may take place every day, every year, or only once in an animal's lifetime. When they migrate, some sea creatures move just a few metres, while others may travel thousands of kilometres across the sea.

Journey to the Sea

Salmon breed in rivers of Europe and North America. The females lay their eggs in holes that the fish dig with their tails. Once they hatch, the baby salmon spend their first years in the river. Eventually, the young fish move down to the sea, where they spend several more years.

When they are ready to breed themselves, the salmon migrate back to the same river where they were born. Here they start the whole process all over again.

Salmon

Going with the Flow

Many animals that live on the shore, such as limpets, move about only when the tide is in. But lots of others, such as bass, stay close to the water's edge, moving up the shore when the tide comes in and moving out to sea when the tide goes out.

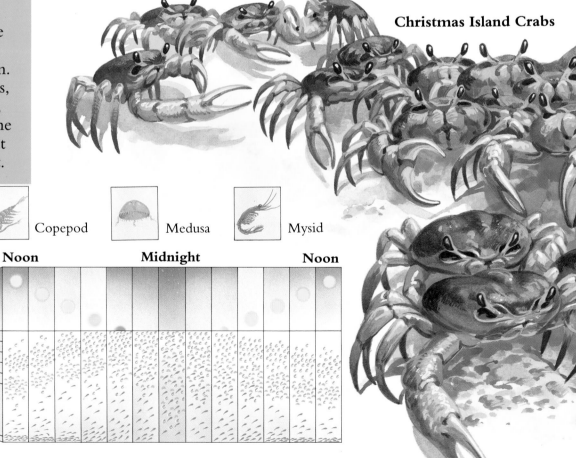

Christmas Island Crabs

Daily Migrations

Many plankton animals swim up towards the surface at night and move down during the day. Most move up and down about 30 m (98 ft), but some move up to 600 m (2,000 ft). This may be so that they can feed safely in the rich surface layers, hidden from their enemies by the darkness.

Copepod   Medusa   Mysid

Noon   Midnight   Noon

Born Ashore

Marine turtles spend most of their lives swimming at the surface of the sea. But female turtles come ashore, often on tropical islands, to lay their eggs. They crawl up the beach and bury their eggs in the sand, sometimes several hundred at a time.

Once the baby turtles hatch, they have to crawl back down to the sea. This journey is very dangerous. Each year, thousands of baby turtles are eaten by birds and other animals.

Baby Turtles

As soon as they have hatched, baby turtles crawl out of their nests and head straight for the sea.

Yearly Travels

Many sea creatures travel to one particular place each year to breed. During the rest of the year, they spread out over a much bigger area. These migrations are not very obvious, except to fishermen trying to catch a certain kind of fish.

Christmas Island Crabs

Christmas Island is a tiny island in the Indian Ocean. Many strange animals live there, including a crab which lives on the forest floor. Every Christmas, millions of crabs migrate to the shore and give birth to their young.

The baby crabs spend about three weeks floating in the plankton, where many are eaten. But the survivors return to the shores of Christmas Island. Some years, there are so many that they turn the beach bright red.

Journey to Land

Some river eels are born in the middle of the Atlantic Ocean near the Sargasso Sea. They drift in the ocean currents and are carried to the coasts where their parents came from.

The tiny eels swim up the rivers and stay for many years. Then they swim back down to the sea and travel to the breeding grounds, thousands of kilometres away.

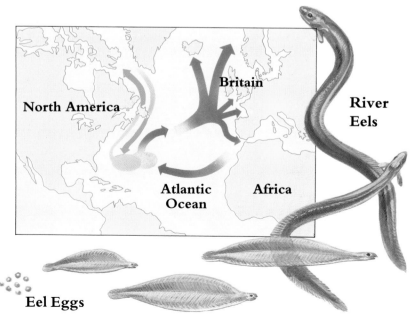

North America

Britain

River Eels

Atlantic Ocean

Africa

Eel Eggs

A Family of Whales

Whales are the largest animals that have ever lived. They are also one of the most intelligent. Although they seem perfectly adapted for life in the sea, whales have not always lived in the water. Millions of years ago, their ancestors lived on land.

Whales returned to the sea at least 65 million years ago. Like human beings, these amazing creatures are warm-blooded mammals that breathe air and nurse their young. They all belong to one of two big groups, toothed whales and whalebone whales.

Blue whales are very powerful swimmers with streamlined bodies.

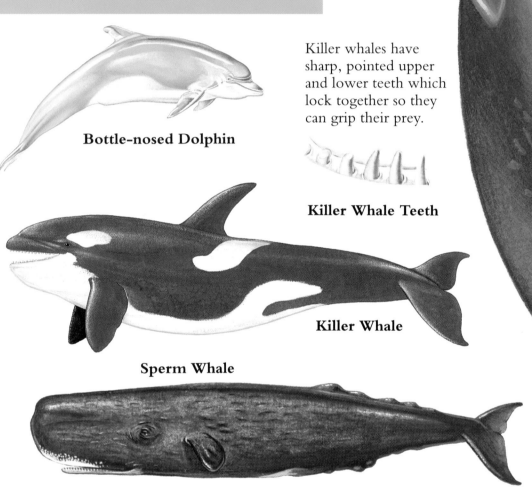

A Toothy Tusk

The toothed whales are by far the largest group. They include all the smaller species, such as dolphins and porpoises, and some larger ones, such as killer whales. Sperm whales are the biggest toothed whales. They may reach a length of 20 m (66 ft) or more.

All toothed whales have cone-shaped teeth, and some dolphins may have as many as 200. Toothed whales mostly eat fish and squid. But killer whales, which grow up to 10 m (33 ft) long, eat penguins, seals, other whales and sometimes people.

Bottle-nosed Dolphin

Killer whales have sharp, pointed upper and lower teeth which lock together so they can grip their prey.

Killer Whale Teeth

Killer Whale

Sperm Whale

Whalebone Whales

Baleen or whalebone whales do not have any teeth at all. Instead of chewing their food, they strain small plankton animals through huge fringed plates, called baleen or whalebone. The plates hang from the roofs of their large mouths.

These gigantic creatures feed mainly during the Summer in the rich waters of the Arctic and Antarctic oceans. During the Winter, some may travel great distances to warmer waters, where they mate and give birth to their young.

Right whales have the longest baleen plates of all. They may grow over 3.6 m (12 ft) long.

Baleen Plate

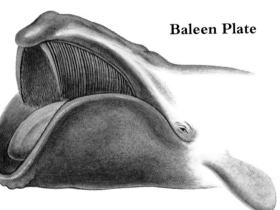

A Spiral Tooth

One of the strangest toothed whales is called a narwhal. It lives in the Arctic parts of the North Atlantic and has only two teeth. In adult males, one of these teeth keeps growing and pierces through the narwhal's top lip, forming a spiral tusk up to 2 m (6.6 ft) long.

Hunting Whales

People have hunted whales for hundreds of years. At first they killed them for the oil in their thick blubber. Today, whale meat is used to make pet food.

When they were chased in sailing ships and hunted with hand-thrown harpoons, only a few whales were killed. But with new harpoon guns and exploding harpoons, many more died each year. So many whales were killed that scientists feared some species would soon become extinct. Now it is illegal to kill certain species of whales.

Today, cannons fire harpoons that were once thrown by hand.

Hand-held Harpoon   **Harpoon Gun**   **Exploding Harpoon**

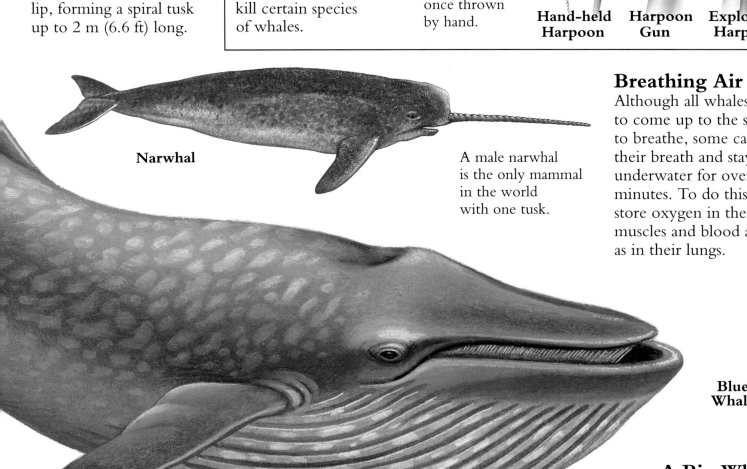

Narwhal

A male narwhal is the only mammal in the world with one tusk.

Blue Whale

Breathing Air

Although all whales have to come up to the surface to breathe, some can hold their breath and stay underwater for over 40 minutes. To do this, they store oxygen in their muscles and blood as well as in their lungs.

The Big Blue Whale

The largest whale of all is the blue whale. It is also the largest animal that has ever lived. It may grow to a length of 30 m (98 ft), and weigh over 150 tonnes.

A blue whale calf weighs about 2 tonnes when it is born. It drinks up to 600 litres (158 gallons) of milk a day, and may double its weight in a week.

A Big Whale's Tiny Food

Although they are so big, blue whales, like the other whalebone whales, feed on tiny plankton animals. In the Antarctic Ocean, blue whales mostly eat little shrimps, called krill, which grow to about 5 cm (2 in). Millions of krill swim together in vast, dense shoals. A large whale may eat more than 2 tonnes of krill in one day.

People and the Sea

For centuries people have been trying to discover more about the sea. Explorers plunge down into the depths in special diving suits and submarines. Scientists study marine life and find new ways to use the sea's resources and to control pollution.

People make use of the sea in many different ways. They get food from it by fishing and farming, oil and gas by drilling the seabed, and minerals by mining the sea floor. But they also use it as a dumping ground for their waste which causes pollution and harms sea life.

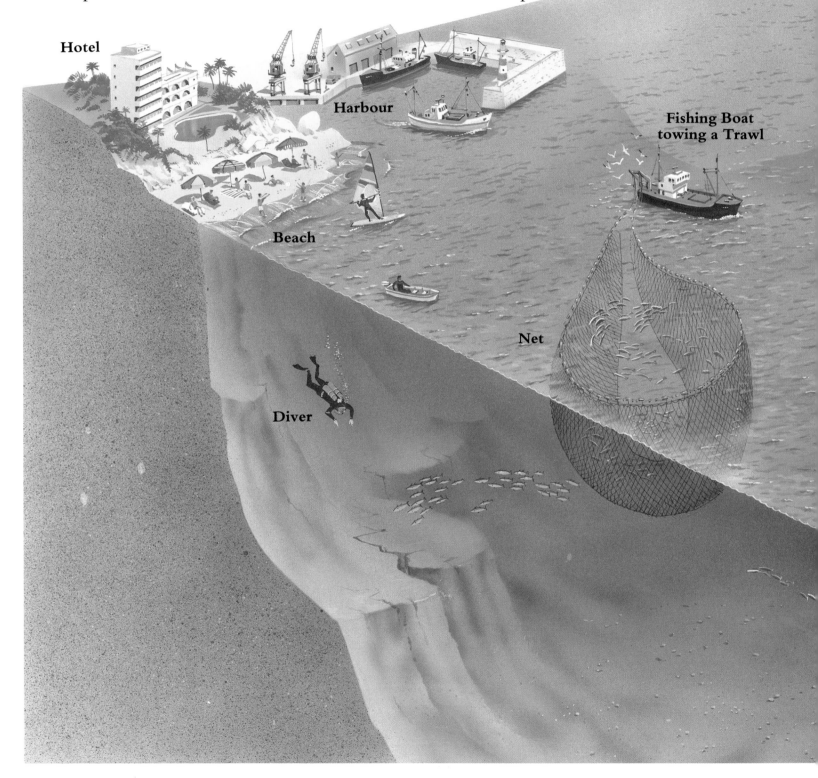

Hotel

Harbour

Beach

Fishing Boat towing a Trawl

Net

Diver

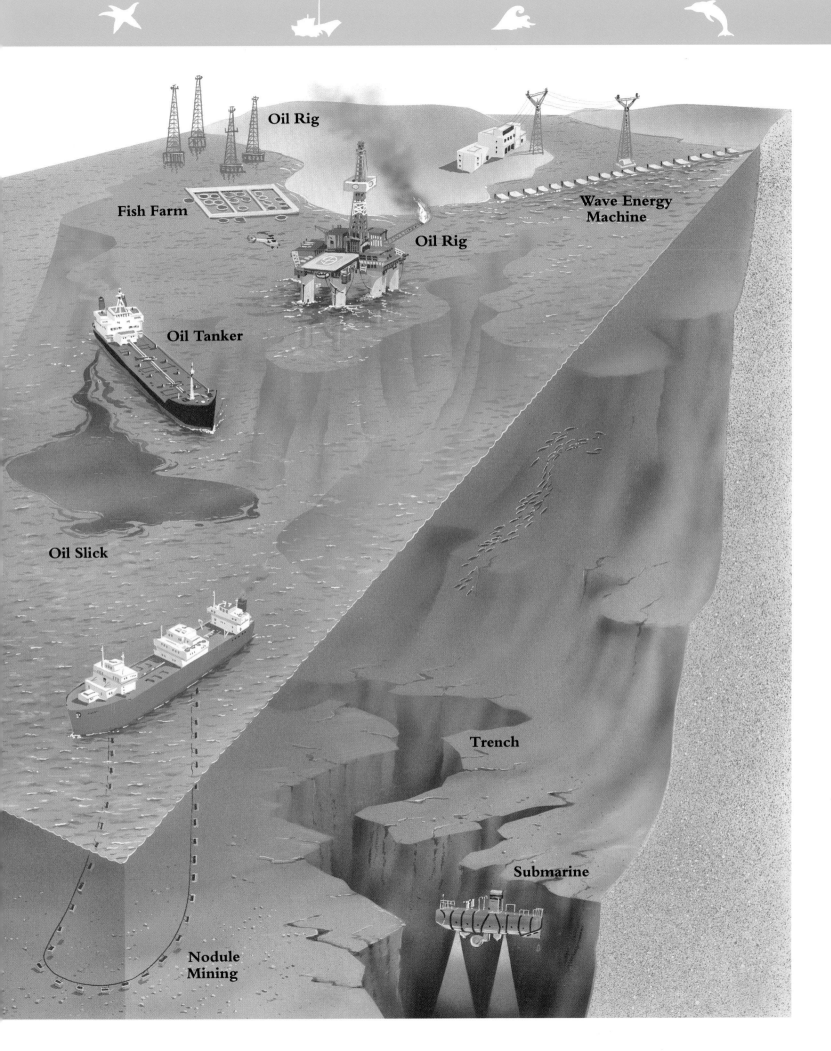

Oil Rig

Fish Farm

Wave Energy
Machine

Oil Rig

Oil Tanker

Oil Slick

Trench

Submarine

Nodule
Mining

Exploring the Oceans

The study of the seas, called oceanography, began in 1872 when a British ship, HMS *Challenger,* sailed from Portsmouth, England, on a three-and-a-half year voyage through the oceans.

Towing plankton nets through the water and trawls across the seabed, scientists and sailors collected deep sea animals that no one had ever seen before. They also lowered thermometers to measure water temperatures.

Scientists at Sea

Scientists still have to go to sea and lower equipment into the ocean. But now they use electronics to collect the information and computers to store and process it. The *Challenger* scientists would be amazed at how fast information can be gathered today.

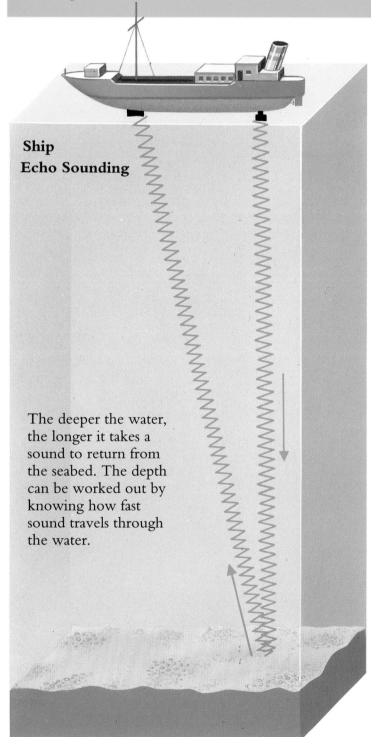

Ship Echo Sounding

The deeper the water, the longer it takes a sound to return from the seabed. The depth can be worked out by knowing how fast sound travels through the water.

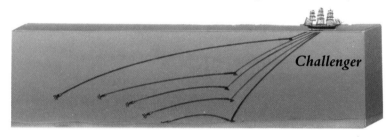

Challenger

Sea Sounds

The *Challenger* scientists measured the ocean depths by lowering a rope with a weight on the end. They measured the length of the rope when the weight hit the bottom. This took many hours. Today, depth is measured by echo sounding. An echo sounder sends a short, sharp, high-pitched sound into the sea. Then it measures the time it takes for the echo to bounce back from the seabed.

Scientists on board HMS *Challenger* used a dredge to collect all kinds of samples from the sea floor.

The Whole Picture

As it moves along, a ship can send out sounds to be measured every few seconds. An echo sounder adds all the results together. It makes a chart showing the shape of the sea floor beneath the ship.

Sound Communication

Scientists use sound for their research because it travels well through water. They place instruments deep in the ocean which send back information using sound signals. Recording instruments are often left anchored to the sea floor for weeks. When a special sound signal is sent from a ship, the connection between the instrument and anchor is broken. Then the instrument floats to the surface to be picked up.

The Sea from Space

Orbiting space satellites send back vast amounts of information to Earth. They may be only 1 km (0.6 miles) above the Earth or as far away as 30,000 km (18,640 miles). Those closest to the Earth can measure the height of waves, as small as 2 cm (0.8 in) high. They can also measure the surface temperature of the ocean and map patches of plankton. Some satellites may even help ships find their way to shore.

Small Submarines

Submersibles are very expensive to build and operate because they need a "mother" ship to take them to and from their diving sites. They are used for scientific research and to inspect and mend underwater cables or oil rigs. Many have mechanical arms that can collect samples or handle tools and cameras. Most can dive down a few hundred metres, but a few can go down to 3,000 m (9,900 ft). A pilot and two passengers travel in the front of the submersible.

Submersible

Mechanical Arm

Diving into the Depths

Divers using Scuba (self-contained underwater breathing apparatus) can go down to 70 m (230 ft) in the sea. They use special gas mixtures to reach depths of 400 m (1,300 ft). Wearing extra-heavy diving suits, they can dive even deeper, up to 500 m (1,640 ft). Below these depths, people explore the sea in miniature submarines, called submersibles.

Scuba

This atmospheric diving suit will work down to depths of 300 m (1,000 ft).

Atmospheric Diving Suit

Scuba divers wear rubber suits and breathe special air which they carry in tanks on their backs.

Fishing

Each year about 70 million tonnes of fish and shellfish are caught in the sea. Large powered ships with all sorts of modern fish-finding and navigation equipment collect most of this harvest.

In poorer parts of the world, people still fish from small sailing boats and use very simple equipment. But no matter how or where fishermen work, it is a very hard and dangerous job.

Fish Nets

Most fish that live on the seabed are caught with large nets, called trawls, that are dragged across the sea floor. A trawl may be held open by a long wooden or metal beam with skids at either end. These are beam trawls.

The biggest trawls do not have a beam. They have two large, flat plates that are dragged ahead of the net. The plates, called otter doors, pull the sides of the net outward and keep the mouth open. This kind of trawl is an otter trawl.

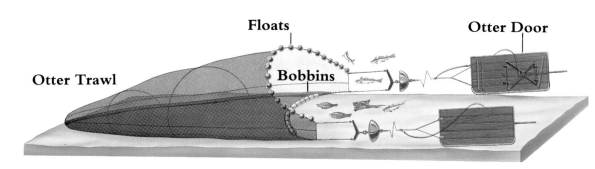

Floats
Otter Door
Otter Trawl
Bobbins

Otter doors open the net from side to side, while floats and bobbins (heavy rollers) open the net from top to bottom.

Hook, Line and Sinker

Some fishermen use lines which are more than 1 km (1.5 miles) long and carry lots of baited hooks to catch fish to sell. They leave the lines on the sea floor attached to big floats at the surface.

One fishing boat will lay many lines before returning to the first one to see what it has caught. Floating longlines, used to catch tuna in the open ocean, may be more than 30 km (19 miles) long.

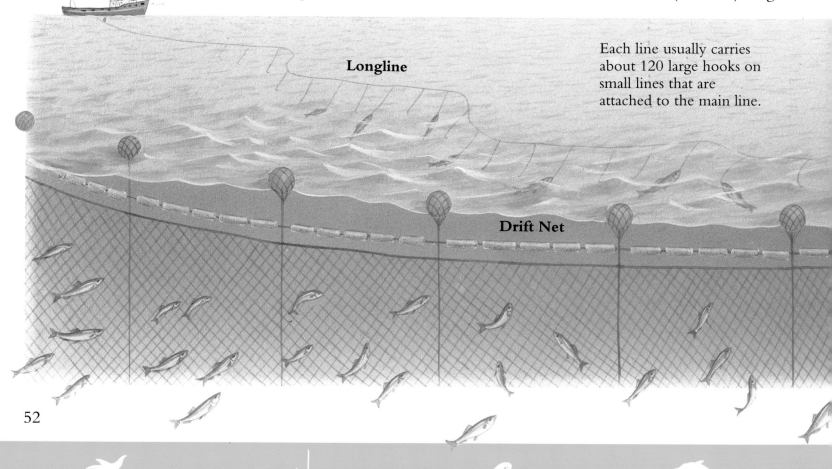

Each line usually carries about 120 large hooks on small lines that are attached to the main line.

Longline

Drift Net

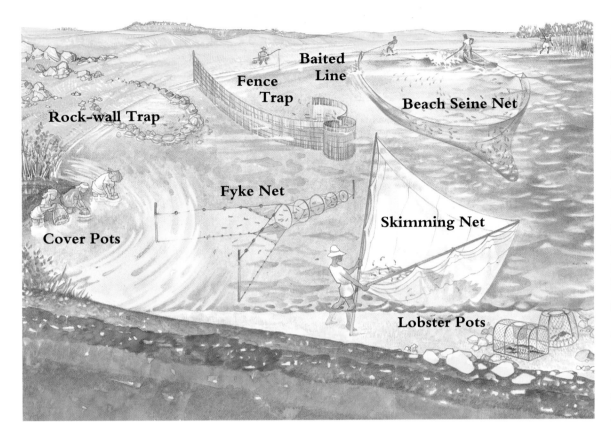

Rock-wall Trap

Fence Trap

Baited Line

Beach Seine Net

Cover Pots

Fyke Net

Skimming Net

Lobster Pots

Fish Ambush

In many parts of the world, fishermen build barriers in shallow water to trap fish as they swim close to the coast. Sometimes they build the traps between the tidemarks so that they can collect the fish when the tide is out. Where the seabed is smooth, they may skim a net across the bottom to catch shrimps and fish.

Trapped!

Fishermen use hundreds of different kinds of baited traps to catch crabs and lobsters, and some types of fish. The traps usually have one or more funnel-shaped openings. A lobster or crab can easily crawl into the trap to eat the bait, but it cannot find its way out again.

Too Many Fish out of Water

Years ago, people thought that there would always be plenty of fish no matter how many were caught. But many parts of the sea have been so overfished that there are now very few fish still living there.

A Dangerous Web

In mid-water, nets are used in a different way. Fine nets, called drift nets, many kilometres long, hang straight down into the water from a row of floats on the surface. Any animal that swims into the net gets tangled up in it. Drift nets are used mainly to catch fish, such as herring and tuna. But the nets also catch and drown seals and whales. Many people believe that drift nets should not be used.

Farming the Seas

Today, it is very difficult for fishermen to earn a living from the sea. Many parts of the ocean have already been so overfished that large shoals of fish are hard to find. Bad weather often prevents fishermen from catching any fish at all.

Instead of fishing, people are now beginning to farm the seas. This is less dangerous and easier to control. Instead of dragging nets through the open seas, people are breeding fish and shellfish in underwater farms just as farmers breed animals on land.

Seaweed Farming

In many parts of the world, especially in China and Japan, people eat seaweed. All kinds of seaweeds have been harvested off the coasts in these areas for hundreds of years. But it is only in this century that people have started farming seaweed to sell.

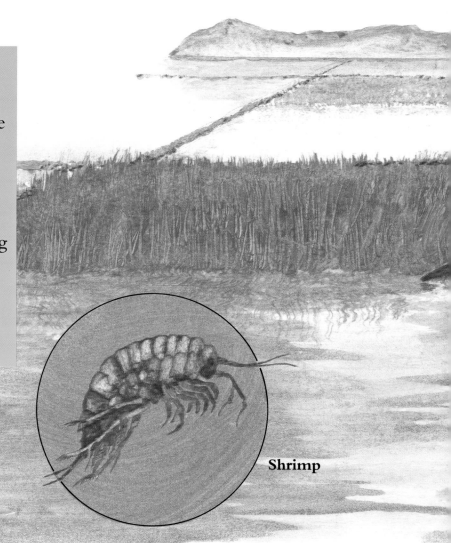

Shrimp

Fish Farming

Freshwater fish farming began thousands of years ago in China. But farming in the sea did not begin until the 1950s. Today, only a few kinds of fish are farmed because it is so expensive.

Only the most valuable fish, such as turbot, trout and salmon, are worth farming. Usually the eggs are hatched in small tanks in hatcheries where the larvae are fed and looked after very carefully. The young fish are then moved into ponds.

Young Trout

Automatic Feeder

Three-year-old Trout

Two-year-old Trout

Fish Farm

Dam

Channel

First Pond

Second Pond

Third Pond

When they are big enough, young trout live in large tanks, where they are fed by an automatic feeder.

When the trout grow bigger, they move into ponds on the fish farm. A dam blocks the river so that water flows to the ponds by a channel.

Water flows back into the river through an opening in each pond.

The first pond is for fish up to one year old. The second is for fish up to two years old and the third pond is for those that are three years old. These fish are kept for breeding.

Paddy Field

During the growing season, paddy fields are always flooded. As the rice grains ripen, the water is slowly drained away.

Salmon Ranches

Salmon lay their eggs in rivers, where they hatch into tiny fish called fry. Salmon ranchers look after the fry until they are old enough to swim back to sea. When the young fish are ready to breed, they swim back to the river where they were born. The ranchers stretch nets across the river to catch the adult fish.

Field of Shrimps

It is very expensive to farm crabs, shrimps and lobsters. Some take years to grow big enough to eat. Warm-water shrimps are the best shellfish to farm because they reach the right size in just a few months.

In hot climates, shrimp farming is often combined with other kinds of farming, such as growing rice. Rice plants grow in shallow ponds called paddy fields. Farmers farm shrimps and fish in the paddy fields.

Shellfish Farming

People have tried to farm shellfish, such as mussels and oysters, since ancient times. The young shellfish grow on tiles or ropes and are given plenty of food out of reach of enemies.

Sometimes adult mussels are kept in tanks until they produce their larvae. The larvae are looked after very carefully and fed on tiny algae, especially grown for them to eat. When they are big enough, the mussels are put into the sea to fatten up, either in cages or under big floating rafts.

Mussels on Ropes

Mussels

55

Resources of the Sea

The seas provide us with all sorts of things that we need to survive and to keep our industries going. Until recently, fish, shellfish and seaweeds were the main resources of the sea, but now many minerals are being found. Oil and gas are two of the most important discoveries, but the greatest resource of all is seawater itself.

Towing Icebergs

Fresh Water from the Sea

One way of taking salt out of seawater to make fresh water is called distillation. Seawater is heated to make steam. The steam is then cooled to turn it back to water, leaving the salt behind.

Another way is to freeze seawater. The ice that forms is fresh because the salt, which does not freeze, is left behind. The ice in icebergs is also fresh. Many years ago, icebergs were towed by ship from the Antarctic to Australia, Africa and South America for their fresh water.

Mining Ship

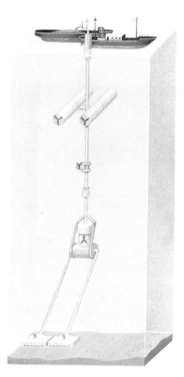

Black Pebbles

In many parts of the world, sand and gravel are scooped up, or dredged, from the seabed to collect all kinds of minerals. Most of these minerals are found near the shore. But one very useful mineral, manganese, is found in much deeper parts of the ocean. Manganese nodules contain many valuable metals, including copper, nickel and cobalt.

The nodules look like small black pebbles. Lying in huge patches on the seabed, they form very slowly, sometimes growing no more than 1 mm every million years. Because they are so deep down, these nodules are too expensive to collect.

One day, ships may mine the depths for manganese nodules by using a special device that picks up nodules from the bottom and pumps them to the surface.

Manganese Nodules

Ocean Facts

About 6 million tonnes of salt are collected from the sea each year.

Sea salt has been used to preserve meat and fish for at least 4,000 years.

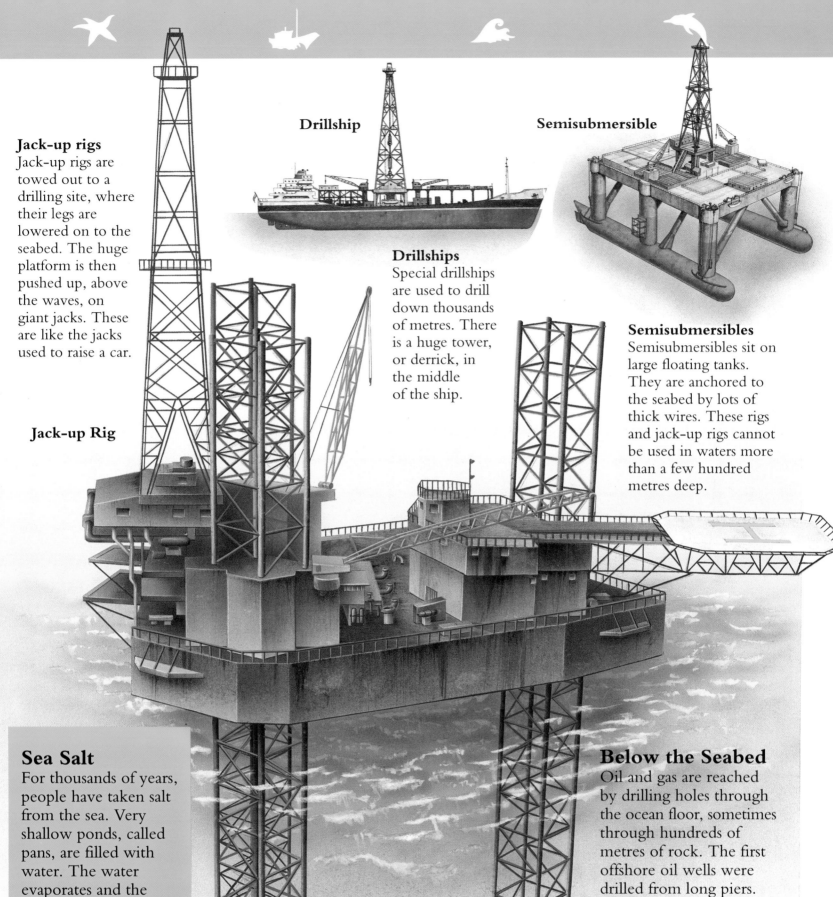

Jack-up rigs
Jack-up rigs are towed out to a drilling site, where their legs are lowered on to the seabed. The huge platform is then pushed up, above the waves, on giant jacks. These are like the jacks used to raise a car.

Jack-up Rig

Drillship

Drillships
Special drillships are used to drill down thousands of metres. There is a huge tower, or derrick, in the middle of the ship.

Semisubmersible

Semisubmersibles
Semisubmersibles sit on large floating tanks. They are anchored to the seabed by lots of thick wires. These rigs and jack-up rigs cannot be used in waters more than a few hundred metres deep.

Sea Salt
For thousands of years, people have taken salt from the sea. Very shallow ponds, called pans, are filled with water. The water evaporates and the ponds dry up, leaving only the salt behind. In very hot places, the water evaporates in the Sun.

Below the Seabed
Oil and gas are reached by drilling holes through the ocean floor, sometimes through hundreds of metres of rock. The first offshore oil wells were drilled from long piers. Since the 1940s, special offshore platforms have been used. The three main types are jack-up rigs, semisubmersibles and drillships.

57

Polluting the Sea

For hundreds of years, people have been throwing their rubbish into the sea. But pollution has only become very serious in the last 50 years. Every day, billions of tonnes of waste, including poisonous chemicals, radioactive waste and plastics, are dumped into the sea. Many towns get rid of human sewage through pipes straight into the sea, and oil tankers wash their tanks in the water. All these things may poison and kill the sea creatures.

Oil Discharge

The Black Menace

Oil causes one of the worst types of pollution in the sea. It comes from leaking oil wells or storage tanks, from oil tankers cleaning their tanks at sea, and from accidental spills when tankers collide with each other or crash into rocks. There are thousands of oil spills every year. Most are small and often not reported.

But some oil spills are huge, covering vast areas of water. Thousands of birds die with their feathers coated in oil, and many kilometres of coastline are smothered with thick, black sludge. Although the oil will eventually be broken down by bacteria in the sea, it can take many years for the marine life to recover.

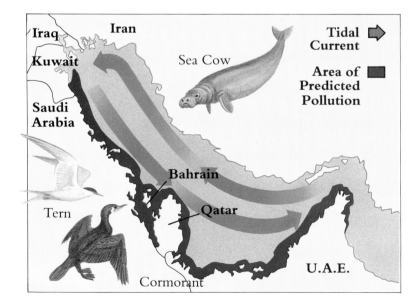

Iraq · Iran · Kuwait · Saudi Arabia · Sea Cow · Bahrain · Qatar · Tern · Cormorant · U.A.E.

Tidal Current →

Area of Predicted Pollution ▇

The Biggest Yet

In February 1991, the biggest oil spill ever recorded poured into the Persian Gulf. It is thought that more than 1.2 million tonnes of oil spilt into the sea. The long-term effects of such a huge spill in the small Persian Gulf are not yet known.

The gulf oil slick was more than twice as big as the disastrous spill from the tanker *Ixtoc* in the Gulf of Mexico. It was also more than 20 times bigger than that of the *Exxon Valdez*. In 1989, a huge oil slick from this tanker caused terrible damage to the coast of Alaska, killing more than 20,000 birds.

Oil Slick

Dirty Shores

If you walk along the shore almost anywhere in the world, you will find all kinds of rubbish mixed in with the seaweed thrown up by wind and waves. Broken bottles, fishing lines, nets and plastic containers often litter the beach. But much more lies under the water.

Thousands of sea birds get tangled up in fishing nets and lines. Turtles, seals and other animals choke after swallowing plastic bags that look like jellyfish. Many plastics do not rot and may stay on the shore for hundreds of years.

Although rubbish on the shore looks bad, it is not as harmful as the pollution in the sea.

There are large amounts of rubbish floating on the surface and rolling about on the seabed.

Invisible Poison

The pollution of the open ocean is much more serious than the rubbish on the shore. Some industries dump dangerous poisons into the sea without even knowing it.

In the 1950s and 1960s, mercury was dumped into the Minamata Bay of Japan. No one thought that the mercury was poisonous, but marine animals converted, or changed, the mercury into a powerful poison. It infected fish and shellfish which were then caught by local fishermen.

Many people ate the polluted shellfish and fish, causing an outbreak of what was later called Minamata disease. The cause was not known for nearly ten years.

The Future of the Oceans

All around the world, people are beginning to realize the importance of the oceans. Laws have now been made in some areas which protect sea animals and stop pollution.

Scientists are discovering new natural resources, new species of fish, and new ways of using the ocean's riches. One day people may even live in cities built out at sea.

Food from the Sea

Before they were hunted, whales of the southern oceans ate about 200 million tonnes of krill each year. But now that there are fewer whales, there are far more krill in the sea. Some experts think that the extra krill, perhaps 150 million tonnes each year, could be taken out of the sea without doing any harm.

Already more than half a million tonnes of krill are caught each year. Most are used to feed animals, but some are made into fish pastes. If the krill industry continues to grow, people all over the world may one day be eating krillfingers and krillburgers.

Model Sea City

City dwellers of the future may find themselves living in a totally new environment — out at sea. Model sea cities are now being researched by scientists.

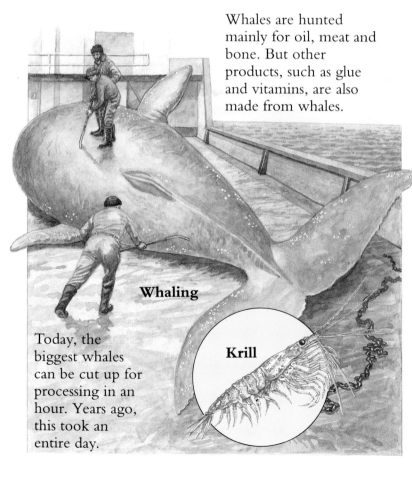

Whales are hunted mainly for oil, meat and bone. But other products, such as glue and vitamins, are also made from whales.

Whaling

Today, the biggest whales can be cut up for processing in an hour. Years ago, this took an entire day.

Krill

Ocean Cities

As the population of the world grows and the land areas become more crowded, it is possible that big cities will be built far out at sea. These would not have to depend on the outside world.

Living Under the Sea

Science fiction writers have often imagined people living in cities under the sea. Special divers already spend days in underwater "houses".

They leave these houses each day to go to work in the sea. They build or mend things under the water, such as oil and gas platforms.

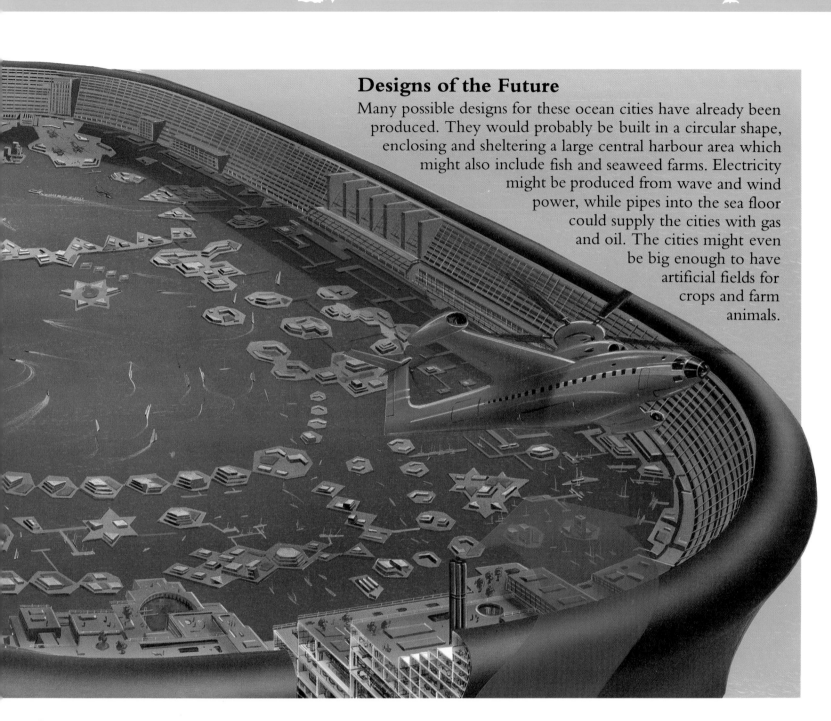

Designs of the Future

Many possible designs for these ocean cities have already been produced. They would probably be built in a circular shape, enclosing and sheltering a large central harbour area which might also include fish and seaweed farms. Electricity might be produced from wave and wind power, while pipes into the sea floor could supply the cities with gas and oil. The cities might even be big enough to have artificial fields for crops and farm animals.

Ocean Power

In the 1980s, offshore oil rigs produced almost a quarter of all the world's oil. But, because there are only limited amounts of oil, other sources of energy are now being developed by scientists.

Some of these involve the oceans, using the energy in waves, tides and currents to produce electricity. One experiment uses floats that bob up and down on the waves. These movements turn the generators which make electricity.

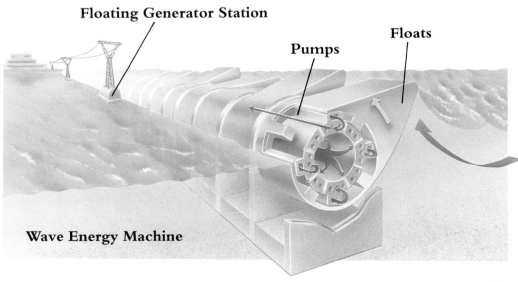

Floating Generator Station

Pumps

Floats

Wave Energy Machine

Glossary

Algae Tiny sea plants with no true roots, stems and leaves.

Bacteria The simplest and smallest living things.

Bony fish Fish that have scaly skins and skeletons made of bone.

Cartilaginous fish Fish that have a skeleton made of cartilage, or gristle, such as sharks and rays.

Continental shelf The shallow part of the oceans around the continents.

Continental slope The steep part of the sea floor joining the continental shelf to the deep sea.

Coral reef The largest living structures on Earth, made of the skeletons of tiny coral animals.

Crustaceans Animals with jointed bodies and limbs, and more than six legs, such as crabs and lobsters.

Currents Streams of water that move through the sea.

Echinoderms Animals with spiny skins and tubed feet, such as starfish and sea urchins.

Equator An imaginary line around the centre of the Earth.

Evaporate To change from a liquid to a gas. Water evaporates when it is heated.

Extinction When one whole species of animal dies out.

Fertilizing chemicals Chemicals that are needed to fertilize plants.

Gas-filled bladder The space inside a plant or animal's body that is filled with gas, like a balloon, to help it float.

Gills The "lungs" of animals that breathe in water. Usually frilly folds of skin filled with blood.

Harbour A safe place for ships to shelter from bad weather and load or unload. May be man-made or natural.

Holdfasts The root-like parts of seaweeds which anchor them to rocks.

Larvae The first stage of life for some animals which looks quite different from the adult stage.

Migration Regular journeys that some animals make to find food and to breed.

Mid-ocean ridges Mountain ranges running under the sea.

Minerals Chemicals found in rocks and the salts dissolved in the sea.

Molluscs Animals with soft bodies usually protected by a hard shell, such as snails, oysters and squid.

Navigation Finding the way from one place to another over the ocean.

Neap tides The smallest tides. They happen twice a month, when the Sun and the Moon pull on the water from different directions.

Plankton Animals and plants that are carried along by ocean currents.

Poles The northern and southern most parts of the Earth.

Radiation Invisible movement of energy – like the heat from the Sun.

Scavengers Animals that feed on waste, including the remains of other animals.

Shellfish A general name that includes both the crustaceans and the molluscs.

Spawn When sea animals release their eggs into the water.

Species One particular kind of animal or plant.

Spring tides The largest tides. They occur when the Sun and Moon both pull on the water from the same direction.

Streamlined Animals with a smooth, even shape that move easily through the water.

Submersibles Small submarines used to explore the sea and to mend oil rigs and underwater cables.

Tides The rise and fall of the sea caused by the pull of the Sun and the Moon.

Trawls Nets that are pulled through the sea to catch fish.

Trenches The very deepest parts of the oceans.

Tropics The warmest parts of the Earth which spread over about 2,000 km (1,240 miles) north and south of the Equator.

Wave The up-and-down movement of the surface of the sea.

Index

algae, 12,30
anchovy, 10,24,55
Antarctic *see* South Pole
Antarctic Circle, 33
Arctic *see* North Pole
Arctic Circle, 32

bacteria, 29,34,35,58
baleen plates, 46
barnacle, 22,23
bear, polar, 32
bioluminescence, 27
bivalve, 11,22
blenny, 23
blubber, 33,47
bonito, 11
brotulid, 11

camouflage, 26,27,36
Caribbean, 6,30
Christmas Island, 45
clam, 21,33,34
  giant, 31
  giant white, 34
coast, 4,13,14,53,58
cockle, 40
cod, 18,25
continental shelf, 4,24,26
continental slope, 4,26
copepod, 16,26
coral, 20,30,31,40
  blue, 30
  brain, 30
  bubble, 30
  colonial, 30
  mushroom, 30
  platform, 30
  tube, 30
coral reef, 10,11,30,31
  Great Barrier Reef,
  30,31
cowfish *see* trunkfish
crab, 10,15,21,22,23,25,
  29,34,41,42,44,53,55
  blind, 34
  hermit, 23,38,41
  Japanese spider, 25

pea, 40
crustacean, 21
current, 4,6,7,12,29,33,
  45,61
  deep sea, 7

defence, 38-39
diver, deep-sea, 51
dogfish, 42
dolphin, 11,46
  bottle-nosed, 46
drift net, 52,53
drillship, 57
dwarf pygmy goby, 18

echo sounder, 50
eel, 10,11
  American, 45
  deep-sea, 10
  European, 45
  gulper, 11
  moray, 31
  river, 45
  snake, 10
environment, 10,36
Exxon Valdez, 58

farming, 48,54-55,61
  fish, 54,61
  salmon, 55
  seaweed, 54,61
  shellfish, 55
fish, angel, 10,30
  angler, 11,27,37
  bat, 10
  bony, 18
  butterfly, 10,31
  cartilaginous, 18,19
  cold-water, 25
  flashlight, 27
  flatfish, 10,17
  flying, 10
  hatchet, 11,27
  lantern, 11,27
  lantern, Risso's, 27
  largest, 19
  moonfish, 19

parrot, 31
pilot, 40
pipefish, 18
puffer, 31
swordfish, 10
tripod, 11,28
trunkfish, 31
viper, 27
fishing, 48,52-53
  net, 12,52,53,59
flatfish, 10,17
flounder, 17

gas, 48,56,57
goblin's kidneys, 6
gold, 5
great swallower, 26
Gulf Stream, 6

haddock, 25
hake, 25
halosaur, 10
harbour, 9,61
herring, 18,24,25,42,52

ice, 4,32-33
iceberg, 32,56
island, 4,24,30
isopod, 11
Ixtoc, 58

jack-up rig, 57
jellyfish, 10,16,17
  compass, 17
  lion's mane, 16
  sea wasp, 17

krill, 26,33,47,60

limpet, 10,22,44
  slipper, 16
lobster, 21,53,55
  American spiny, 21
  common, 25
lobster pot, 53

mackerel, 10,24,42

mammal, 25,46-47
marlin, 10
Mediterranean, 9
mercury, 59
migration, 44
Minamata Bay, 59
minerals, 48,56,60
  cobalt, 56
  copper, 56
  manganese, 56
  nickel, 56
Moon, 8,9
  and tides, 8,9
moonfish, 19
mudskipper, 37
mussel, 10,22,23,33,38,
  40,55

narwhal, 47
North Pole, 4,6,32
nutrient, 24

ocean, 4-5
  and sunlight, 5,12,27,30
  and temperature, 5-6
  and wind, 4,6,7,23
  Antarctic, 7,32-33,46,
  47,56
  Arctic, 6,7,32-33,46
  Atlantic, 24,32,45
  depth, 4,5
  Indian, 30,32,40
  Pacific, 30,32,40
  power from, 61
  Southern, 32,33
ocean city, 61
oceanography, 50,51
octopus, 10
oil, 49,56,57,58,60
  slick, 58,59
  tanker, 58
  well, 57,58
oyster, 38,40

parasite, 40
partnership, 40-41
penguin, 33,46

periwinkle, 23
Persian Gulf, 58
pilchard, 24
pipefish, 18
plaice, 17
plankton, 11,12,13,16-17,18,
  19,20,24,30,33,42,44,46,47
poison, 13,15,17,21,31,39,
  58,59
pollution, 48,58,59,60
polyp, 30
porpoise, 11,46
Portuguese man-of-war,
  10,15
prawn, 23
  luminous, 26

rat tail, 10
ray, 10,19,40
  electric, 19,39
  torpedo, 39
razor shell, 21
Red Sea, 30
reef see coral reef
remora, 41
rock pool, 23

sail-by-the-wind, 15
salmon, 44,54
  ranch, 55
salt, 45,56
sand dollar, 10
sandhopper, 23
sardine, 24
Sargasso Sea, 14,45
scallop, 10,21
scavenger, 29
  shrimp, 29
sea anemone, 10,20,21,22,
  23,30,31,34,39,40,41
  snakelocks, 31
sea cucumber, 10,11,29,38
  cotton-spinner, 38
sea fan, 31
sea horse, 10,18,19,36
  Australian, 36
sea lily, 28
sea pen, 10,20
sea slug, 10,23,39
sea spider, 10

sea urchin, 10,16,20,23,
  29,38,41
sea whip, red, 30,31
seabed, 10,17,19,
  20-21,25,26,28,29,34,
  35,39,43,48,56,59
seal, 32,33,46,53,59
  Antarctic, 33
  Arctic, 32
  crab-eater, 33
  elephant, 33
  leopard, 33
  ringed, 32
  Ross, 33
  Weddell, 33
seashore, 6,13,15,22,23,44,
  45,59
seawater, 5,56
seaweed, 10,12-13,14,18,
  22,23,54,56,59
  bladder wrack, 13
  carragheen, 13
  farming, 54,61
  furbelows, 12
  giant kelp, 12
  holdfast, 13,22
  kelp, 12
  Plocamium, 12
  Sargassum weed, 15
  serrated wrack, 12
  sugar kelp, 12
  thongweed, 13
semisubmersible, 57
shark, 10,11,19,37,40,
  41,42-43
  basking, 42
  blue, 43
  dwarf Pacific, 42
  great white, 42,43
  hammerhead, 43
  largest, 19
  mako, 19
  nurse, 42
  sand, 43
  spurdog, 10
  squaloid, 37
  thresher, 42
  tiger, 43
  whale, 18,19,42
  white-tip, 11,19

shell, cone, 31
  top, 10
shellfish, 31,52,54,56,59
shoal, 24,25,31,42,43,54
shore, 6,13,15,22,44,45,59
shrimp, 14,15,21,23,26,27,
  29,33,34,40,42,53,55
  cleaner, 41
  pistol, 39
  warm-water, 40,55
skate, 19
snail, 16,29,42
  Ianthina, 15
snake, 36
  banded, 36
  flat, 36
snapper, glasseye, 10
South Pole, 4,6,32
sponge, 10,16,20,31
  chalice, 20
  loggerhead, 20
  pottery, 20
springs, hot water, 34-35
squid, 10,11,19,25,33,46
  deep-sea, 11
  giant, 25
  vampire, 10
stalked crinoids, 10
starfish, 10,11,16,20,22,
  28,31,38
  brittle star, 10
  feather star, 28
  red, 16,38
  short-armed, 11
stomatoid, 10
Strait of Gibraltar, 9
submarine, 49
submersible, 51
Sun, 4,8,9,23
  and tides, 8,9

tentacle, 15,16,17,20,21,
  22,39,40,41
tidal range, 9
  highest, 9
tide, 4,8-9,22,44,61
  high, 8,9,22,44
  low, 8,9,44
  neap, 9
  spring, 9

trawl, 52
trawling, 50
trench, 4,5,28
  Marianas, 5
trout, 54
trunkfish, 31
tube-feet, 21
tuna, 24,52
  albacore, 11
  bluefin, 24
turbot, 54
turtle, 10,14,41,45,59
  green, 10
  leatherback, 14
twilight zone, 26-27

underwater mountain
  range, 4,5

vent, hot water, 34-35
Venus flower basket, 10
volcano, 5

walrus, 32
wave, 4,6,7,13,14,22,61
  biggest, 6
  freak, 6
  surface, 6
whale, 10,32,33,46-47,
  53,60
  baleen, 46-47
  blue, 11,46,47
  killer, 46
  right, 46
  sperm, 11,46
  toothed, 46-47
whalebone see baleen
whelk, dog, 38
whiting, 25
worm, 10,16,21,23,31,34,
  35,41,42
  annelid, 16
  arrow, 16
  bottom-dwelling, 10
  burrowing, 29
  fan, 21
  keel, 21
  lugworm, 23
  rag, 21
  tube, 35